Rhetoric & Composition
PhD Program

PROGRAM
Pioneering program honoring the rhetorical tradition through scholarly innovation, excellent job placement record, well-endowed library, state-of-the-art New Media Writing Studio, and graduate certificates in new media and women's studies.

TEACHING
1-1 teaching loads, small classes, extensive pedagogy and technology training, and administrative fellowships in writing program administration and new media.

FACULTY
Nationally recognized teacher-scholars in history of rhetoric, modern rhetoric, women's rhetoric, digital rhetoric, composition studies, and writing program administration.

FUNDING
Generous four-year graduate instructorships, competitive stipends, travel support, and several prestigious fellowship opportunities.

EXPERIENCE
Mid-sized liberal arts university setting nestled in the vibrant, culturally-rich Dallas-Fort Worth metroplex.

English
DEPARTMENT

Contact Dr. Mona Narain
m.narain@tcu.edu
eng.tcu.edu

Manuscript Reviewers 2019

Sara P. Alvarez
Ann Blakeslee
Casey Boyle
Kevin Brock
David Coogan
Jacob Craig
Gita DasBender
Danielle DeVoss
Sidney Dobrin
Christiane Donahue
Doug Downs
Dana Lynn Driscoll
Dylan Dryer
Abby Dubisar
John Duffy
Bryna Siegel Finer
Lynee Gaillet
Christopher Garcia
Laurie Grobman
Holly Hassel
Kristine Johnson
Alison Knoblauch
Steve Lamos
Neal Lerner
Rory Lee
William Maccauley
Rita Malenczyk
Loren Marquez
Christine Martorana
Stephen McElroy

Dan Melzer
Michelle Miley
Susan Miller-Cochran
Lilian Mina
Jessie Moore
Kelly A. Moreland
Tracy Morse
Jessica Nastal-Dema
Timothy Oleksiak
Peggy O'Neill
Lori Ostergaard
Justine Post
Annette Powell
Jessica Restaino
Andrea Riley-Mukavetz
Kelly Ritter
Shelley Rodrigo
Phyllis Mentzell Ryder
David Sheridan
Steve Sherwood
Ryan Skinnell
Erec Smith
Cindy Tekobbe
Darci Thoune
Christine Tulley
Kate Vieira
Stacey Waite
Jennifer Wingard
Erin Workman
Kathleen Yancey

composition STUDIES

Volume 48, Number 1
Spring 2020

Editors
Matthew Davis
Kara Taczak

Editorial Consultant
Bob Mayberry

Book Review Editor
Bryna Siegel Finer

Editorial Assistants
Megan Busch
Wafaa Razeq

Former Editors
Gary Tate
Robert Mayberry
Christina Murphy
Peter Vandenberg
Ann George
Carrie Leverenz
Brad E. Lucas
Jennifer Clary-Lemon
Laura R. Micciche

Advisory Board
Sheila Carter-Tod
 Virginia Tech University

Elías Dominguez Barajas
 University of Arkansas

Qwo-Li Driskill
 Oregon State University

Susan Martens
 Missouri Western State University

Aja Y. Martinez
 Syracuse University

Michael McCamley
 University of Delaware

Jessica Nastal-Dema
 Prairie State College

Annette Harris Powell
 Bellarmine University

Melissa Berry Pearson
 Northeastern University

Margaret Price
 The Ohio State University

Jessica Restaino
 Montclair State University

Donnie Sackey
 The University of Texas at Austin

Christopher Schroeder
 Northeastern Illinois University

Darci Thoune
 University of Wisconsin-La Crosse

SUBSCRIPTIONS

Composition Studies is published twice each year (May and November). Annual subscription rates: Individuals $25 (Domestic), $30 (International), and $15 (Students). To subscribe online, please visit *https://compstudiesjournal.com/subscriptions/* https://compstudiesjournal.com/subscriptions/.

BACK ISSUES

Back issues, five years prior to the present, are freely accessible on our website: https://compstudiesjournal.com/archive/. If you don't see what you're looking for, contact us. Also, recent back issues are now available through Amazon.com. To find issues, use the advanced search feature and search on "Composition Studies" (title) and "Parlor Press" (publisher).

BOOK REVIEWS

Assignments are made from a file of potential book reviewers. If you are interested in writing a review, please contact our Book Review editor at brynasf@iup.edu.

JOURNAL SCOPE

The oldest independent periodical in the field, *Composition Studies* publishes original articles relevant to rhetoric and composition, including those that address teaching college writing; theorizing rhetoric and composing; administering writing programs; and, among other topics, preparing the field's future teacher-scholars. All perspectives and topics of general interest to the profession are welcome. We also publish Course Designs, which contextualize, theorize, and reflect on the content and pedagogy of a course. CFPs, announcements, and letters to the editor are most welcome. *Composition Studies* does not consider previously published manuscripts, unrevised conference papers, or unrevised dissertation chapters.

SUBMISSIONS

For submission information and guidelines, see https://compstudiesjournal.com/submissions/.

Direct all correspondence to:

> Matthew Davis, Co-Editor
> Department of English
> UMass Boston
> 100 Morrissey Blvd
> Boston MA 02125–3393
> compstudiesjournal@gmail.com

Composition Studies is grateful for the support of the University of Massachusetts Boston and the University of Denver.

© 2020 by Matthew Davis and Kara Taczak, Co-Editors

Production and distribution is managed by Parlor Press, www.parlorpress.com.

ISSN 1534–9322.

Cover art by Jody Shipka.

https://compstudiesjournal.com/

composition STUDIES

Volume 48, Number 1
Spring 2020

Contents

Manuscript Reviewers 2019	4
From the Editors: In Times of Trouble	9

At a Glance: Connections & Collaborations

Developing Writers in Higher Education: A Longitudinal Study   14
    Anne Ruggles Gere, Laura Aull, Gail Gibson, Lizzie Hutton, Benjamin Keating, Anna V. Knutson, Ryan McCarty, Justine Post, Naomi Silver, Sarah Swofford, Emily Wilson

Articles

Self-Authorship and Faculty Writers' Trajectories of Becoming   16
    Sandra L. Tarabochia

Career Killer Survival Kit: Centering Single Mom Perspectives in Composition and Rhetoric   34
    Alex Hanson

Affirming Difference: Inhabiting the WPA Otherwise   53
    Nathaniel Street

Politeness Profiles in the First-Year Composition Classroom   71
    Pennie L. Gray

Course Designs

Eng 7980: Learning Transfer in *History and Theories of Composition*   88
    Ryan P. Shepherd, David T. Johnson, Sue Fletcher, Courtney A. Mauck, and Christopher J. Barber

English 391ml: Multilingualism and Literacy in Western Mass   103
    Rebecca Lorimer Leonard, Kyle Piscioniere, Danielle Pappo

Where We Are

Networking Undergraduate Research: Where We Are,
Where We Can Go 115
    Dominic DelliCarpini and Jessie L. Moore

Theorizing with Undergraduate Researchers 119
    Kristine Johnson and J. Michael Rifenburg

Inexperience and Innovation 121
    Courtney Buck, Emily Nolan, and Jamie Spallino

Multimedia Undergraduate Research in Composition 124
    Hannah Bellwoar, Jill Palmer, and Fisher Stroud

Book Reviews

Social Media Ethics and the Rhetorical Tradition 127
Rhetoric, Technology, and the Virtues, by Jared S. Colton and Steve Holmes
Social Writing/Social Media: Publics, Presentations, and Pedagogies,
edited by Douglas M. Walls and Stephanie Vie
    Reviewed by Kristine L. Blair

Re/Orienting Writing Studies: Queer Methods, Queer Projects,
edited by William P. Banks, Matthew B. Cox, and Caroline Dadas 136
    Reviewed by Katrina L. Miller

Serendipity in Rhetoric, Writing, and Literacy Research,
edited by Maureen Daly Goggin and Peter N. Goggin 141
    Reviewed by Michael Pak

*Black Perspectives in Writing Program Administration: From the
Margins to the Center,* edited by Staci M. Perryman-Clark
and Colin Lamont Craig 145
    Reviewed by Floyd Pouncil

Rhetorical Feminism and This Thing Called Hope, by Cheryl Glenn 149
    Reviewed by Anne Turner

Next Steps: New Directions for/in Writing about Writing,
edited by Barbara Bird, Doug Downs, I. Moriah McCracken,
and Jan Rieman 153
    Reviewed by John H. Whicker

Contributors 157

From the Editors: In Times of Trouble

Greetings & Reflections

We welcome you—warmly!—to our spring 2020 issue. And we do so, again, with gratitude. First, with thanks for our new editorial assistant, Megan J. Busch, a doctoral candidate at the University of South Carolina. Joining Wafaa Razeq as one of our editorial assistants, Megan brings an infectious energy and unmatched organizational strategies, both of which are welcome and needed additions to our team. Additionally, we would like to take this opportunity to thank Emmy Boes and Nick Marsellas, both of whom have cycled off the editorial team, for their help with the fall issue. In addition, you will find a list of reviewers from 2019 in the final pages of the journal. We'd like to express our deepest gratitude to all of them: the journal relies on the dedicated, thorough, and unremunerated work of reviewers; it is reviewers that ensure that potential authors receive helpful and encouraging feedback. If you would like to join them and review for *Composition Studies*, please drop us a line (compstudiesjournal@gmail.com).

Reflecting in and on this moment brings forth feelings of uncertainty, trauma, and fear. We sit writing this editorial with the United States in the grip of more than two months of stay-at-home guidance brought on by the COVID-19 pandemic. During this time, daily life has been dramatically re-shaped, and new terminology has entered the popular lexicon: social distancing, PPE, Zoom, asymptomatic transmission, community spread, contact tracing, case fatality rate.

As we physically distance ourselves from family, friends, students, and colleagues, avoid trips out as much as possible, and slog through online video conference after online video conference, many parents also balance the Herculean task of caring for children day after day, hosting school from the living room or kitchen, and maintaining professional duties. Others of us attempt to care for at-risk and ill family and friends. All of this work happens amidst mass mis- and dis-information campaigns, and in the context of empirically verified unequal distribution of resources (and illness) across lines of race, class, and gender, and alongside furloughs and layoffs embedded within the exponentially increased unemployment numbers serving as a harbinger of the uncertain times for colleges and universities facing budgetary and enrollment shortfalls that nearly guarantee to shutter some campuses. And, at least as of this moment, it seems that this litany simply foretells coming economic instability (or collapse) and the continued effects of catastrophic climate change.

In short, the COVID-19 pandemic has us in a time of trouble. And though we do not mean this introduction as a lament, there is no doubt that various parts of our individual and collective well-being are challenged, compromised, and threatened.

In 1912, Edwin Hopkins asked, "Can composition be taught under the current conditions?" – and his answer was "no." Yet, here we are. Composition instructors have long been teaching in crisis. And, in fact, we are a discipline that understands how to work in uncertain times. From crisis came the robust anti-racist, feminist, and anti-discriminatory work that our field continues to pursue. From crisis came our attunement to labor, in all its forms—domestic, professional, civil, and otherwise. From crisis came our histories, methods and methodologies, programs, theories, and pedagogies. We know how to be effective teachers, even—maybe especially—in crisis. It is one reason that our colleagues in other disciplines and departments come to us—to our writing centers and writing programs and digital studios—in times of need. Explicitly or not, students and faculty recognize expertise: they see that we know how to talk about pedagogy, can help with assignment building, can problem solve technological issues, and can back it up with research besides.

Perhaps that is part of why the networks of support in our discipline are so sturdy. Through channels formal and informal, we already see members of the discipline seeking to be a light for our families, loved ones, each other, and colleagues, as well as our students. From virtual workshops to online conferences, from extended Zoom office hours to backchannel check-ins, we notice everywhere small (and large!) efforts to ease a difficult moment. Take a quick glance at social media platforms and you will find colleagues from across the country extending themselves to help one another. Have a question? Feeling unmotivated? Stressed or overwhelmed? Need a pick-me-up or a brief bit of joy? Folks in writing and rhetoric, it seems, are standing by. These platforms, and others, continue to provide networks of support, connecting many people in our discipline when we need it most.

As we navigate these uncertain times, we know our work as educators offers a sense of stability to students; our programs create communities oriented toward better, more just futures; and our scholarship provides a way of negotiating meaning in a tumultuous world.

Points of Continuity

In the process of trying to understand and reflect on the current moment, we have found ourselves lifted up by small bits of continuity. One such bit has been continued work on the journal's infrastructure.

For instance, this issue includes a new section: At a Glance: Connections & Collaborations. We see this section as a place for collaborative research studies in the field to present their work—on methods and methodologies, data, results, and implications—in visual form. This section will celebrate the work we do collaboratively, and we welcome—borrowing loosely from Johanna Drucker's *Graphesis: Visual Forms of Knowledge Production*—visual representations, interpretations, and knowledge-making graphics. If you and your collaborator(s) would like to be featured in this section, we welcome inquiries via email!

One of our goals for the journal was to build out the online and social media presence, and with the release of the spring issue, we have begun to do just that. First, the *CS* website has moved to a WordPress site, and as an independent journal, our hope is it will be the permanent location. Some other changes include new house style guidelines, a new logo, and even new fonts. As we mentioned in our fall editorial, the website will also house all of the Course Design syllabi and ancillary materials; we hope this will allow easier access and open space for creative composition of those documents. The new website can be found at: https://compstudiesjournal.com/ We are also on Instagram (compstudiesjournal) and Twitter (@CompStudiesJrnl), and both are actively maintained.

Lastly, in summer 2020, we will release our first special issue on corequisite writing courses specifically addressing equity, access, and institutional change. Our guest editors, Heidi Estrem, Dawn Shepherd, and Samantha Sturman have been hard at work and gearing up for this issue. It will be released fully online on our website. We are also seeking collaborative editorial teams for summer 2021, so if you have a possible topic, please submit a proposal to <compstudiesjournal@gmail.com>

This Issue

This spring issue offers a number of exciting pieces, including the cover, which Jody Shipka designed. We're grateful for her work in composing an image that, for us, simultaneously evokes the history of text technologies, the domesticity of our current moment, and the ways the two often intersect with gender. Her cover appears in her characteristic assemblage style and with dedication to detail. Those are, we feel compelled to mention, homemade and hand-decorated *Composition Studies* cookies.

At a Glance: Connections & Collaboration

We are thrilled that Anne Gere, Laura Aull, Gayle Gibson, Laurie Hutton, Benjamin Keating, Anne Knutson, Ryan McCarty, Justine Post, Naomi Silver, Sarah Swofford, and Emily Wilson accepted our offer to compose the inaugural piece for this section. Their infographical diptych represents the collaborative longitudinal research in their recently published and co-authored *Developing Writers in Higher Education*.

The Articles

The issue begins with Sandra Tarabochia's interview-based longitudinal study of faculty writers, which sounds the call to see faculty as both authors and self-authors, as writers who deserve support in the long arc of inventing and reinventing themselves anew. Next, Alex Hanson's piece provides a necessary and timely analysis that focuses attention on the experiences of single mothers in rhetoric and composition. In addition to exploring a "career killer survival kit" for single mothers in the discipline, her piece ends with suggestions for change at organizational, institutional, and departmental levels, and a generous appendix for those interested in further resources. Nathaniel Street's "Affirming Difference" is an exploration of the subject-position of WPA that draws on a wide range of theoretical frameworks to urge administrators to open spaces of similarity and difference through disidentification, multiplicity, intersection, and "not-knowing." Finally, Pennie Gray's empirical study documents and theorizes student pushback to giving critical feedback within peer review activity contexts. Gray finds that students' practices of negotiating social space and linguistic face form discursive patterns; understanding these patterns, which she identifies as "politeness profiles," can lead to improved peer review activity design and implementation.

The Course Designs

This issue's course designs focus on graduate and upper-level undergraduate courses, and both represent departures from traditional approaches to theory, history, and community engagement. In a course design co-authored with graduate students, Ryan Shepherd traces the transformation of a graduate course in composition theory and history into a Teaching for Transfer course. Through multifaceted reflections, the authors trace how their theories of writing became, simultaneously, theories of the discipline; share the 11 questions that framed their engagement throughout the course; and suggest possible tweaks to the course. Rebecca Lorimer Leonard and her co-authors find that redesigning an upper-level, undergraduate Writing About Writing course helps them engage more deeply with literacy scholarship on multilingualism and community engagement.

The Where We Are Section

This issue's Where We Are focuses on an issue in the field near and dear to us: undergraduate research (UR) in composition studies. We are pleased at the number and range of voices that agreed to contribute to the section. To begin, Dominic DelliCarpini and Jessie Moore provide a quick but rich history of UR's networks and institutions. Kristine Johnson and J. Michael Rifenburg then outline the ways that UR can continue to attend to accessibility, including more specific attention to including student voices. Answering their call are the students themselves: Courtney Buck, Emily Nolan, and Jamie Spallino, all undergraduate students, outline their longitudinal research project for Wittenberg University's Writing Center. Tracing their research process from inexperience to expertise, they quite literally "come to terms" with writing center research through innovation, hard work, and friendship. Finally, Hannah Bellwoar, Jill Palmer, and Fisher Stroud from Juniata College provide a multiperspectival reflection on multimedia UR, finding that, for faculty and students alike, the key to successful UR is starting early, negotiating roles, encouraging one another, pushing at perceived boundaries, and allowing students the freedom to "combine their interests with their coursework and pursue research in multiple media to reach the audiences that matter to them."

The Book Reviews

The book reviews commence with Kristine Blair's insightful, capacious review essay in which she overviews two new volumes on rhetorical study of social media; in doing so, she helps us see the way both books position the multiplicities of social networks as a "vital continuation" of rhetoric's historical roots in the study of ethical frameworks. Similarly, the other reviews make and build on important connections in the field: queerness and methodology, serendipity and writing research, race and WPA work, rhetorical study and feminism, and students and faculty reflecting on Writing about Writing pedagogy.

Stay safe. Be well.

MD and Kt
Boston, MA and Denver, CO
May 2020

At a Glance: Connections & Collaborations

DEVELOPING WRITERS IN HIGHER EDUCATION: A LONGITUDINAL STUDY

ANNE RUGGLES GERE, EDITOR

KEY FINDINGS

Writing development is non-linear, multifaceted, and complex. The transformative effects of college writing are marked by unevenness and are not always visible. Writing development emerges from students' critical engagement with curricula and processes of writing and is tightly intertwined with personal and social development. As the lists to the right show, writing development is shaped by students' life experiences, personal attributes, and writing experiences.

- All Writers Have More to Learn
- Genre Awareness Contributes to Writing Development
- Writing is a Rhetorical and Social Activity
- Writing Development Precedes and Extends Beyond College
- Writing Benefits from Attention to Language-Level Features

CONTRIBUTING AUTHORS

LAURA L. AULL · ANNE RUGGLES GERE · GAIL GIBSON · LIZZIE HUTTON · BENJAMIN KEATING · ANNA V. KNUTSON · RYAN MCCARTY · JUSTINE POST · NAOMI SILVER · SARAH SWOFFORD · EMILY WILSON

EXPLORE THE E-BOOK & DATASET
https://doi.org/10.3998/mpub.10079890

- 169 students across seven years
  - 60 writing minors, 109 non-minors
  - 137 women, 32 men
  - 47 different majors
- 4,225 demographic data points
- 322 pre-/post-surveys
- 131 pre-/post-interviews
- 2,406 writing artifacts

Case Studies · Corpus Linguistics · Digital Analysis · Grounded Coding · Statistical Analysis · Textual Analysis

LIFE EXPERIENCES

- College
- Community
- Extracurricular
- Family
- High School
- Relationships
- Work

PERSONAL ATTRIBUTES

- Agency
- Conceptions of Writing
- Expectations
- Goals and Motivations
- Identities
- Personal Development
- Self-Efficacy

WRITING EXPERIENCES

- Digital Writing
- Disciplinary Experiences
- Instructor Feedback
- Peer Review
- Writing Assignments
- Reading
- Reflection and Self-Assessment

VISIT THE COMPANION SITE
https://www.developingwritersbook.org/

INFOGRAPHIC BY: JUSTINE POST · SARAH SWOFFORD · LIZZIE HUTTON · ANNA V. KNUTSON · NAOMI SILVER · ANNE RUGGLES GERE

Articles

Self-Authorship and Faculty Writers' Trajectories of Becoming

Sandra L. Tarabochia

Writing researchers know relatively little about the needs and experiences of faculty writers. As a result, institutional approaches to improving scholarly productivity fail to account for vital components of writerly development and in doing so limit access to the academic enterprise. Drawing on an interview-based longitudinal study of faculty writers and the construct of self-authorship from the field of human development, this article reveals epistemological, interpersonal and intrapersonal dimensions of faculty writer development. Invoking Paul Prior, I call for inclusive support strategies that acknowledge and sponsor faculty writers' complex trajectories of becoming.

In her 2017 article "Writing by the Book, Writing Beyond the Book," Kristine Johnson urges readers of *Composition Studies* to be "present and persuasive in current conversations about scholarly writing" especially as they relate to graduate student and faculty writers (57). Although writing researchers regularly draw on disciplinary knowledge to inform decisions about undergraduate writing curriculum, pedagogy and assessment, we have "paid virtually no attention to faculty writers" (65). As a result, Johnson argues, popular approaches to supporting faculty writers do not always align with our disciplinary expertise about writing and writer development.

By way of example, Johnson critiques writing advice manuals, such as Paul Silvia's *How to Write a Lot* and Wendy Belcher's *Writing Your Journal Article in Twelve Weeks*, for emphasizing behavior over process and separating the act of writing from rhetorical invention, deep thinking, discovery and knowledge making (61-2).[1] Behavioral strategies for improving writing productivity (e.g., write for 15 minutes a day, write 1000 words a day, do not write in your office), she laments, often treat writing as an "emotionally detached activity" that can be habitualized, even though we know writing involves a wide range of emotion (Johnson 58; Driscoll and Wells; Driscoll and Powell; Gross and Alexander; McLeod; Stenberg). Although behavior-based approaches can have practical, "utilitarian benefits," they "risk putting an exclusive focus on short-term tips and strategies, rather than on long-term processes" (Werder 280). In Johnson's words, they forward an "epistemologically current-traditional" vision of writing and writers that contradicts the "declarative and procedural knowledge about writing" established in composition studies and are therefore limited in "how well and how far they can support scholarly writers" (57, 63).

In response, Johnson calls for empirical studies of graduate student and faculty writers that seek to better understand the "behavioral, emotional, and intellectual challenges in scholarly writing" (67). In this article, I take up her call by sharing preliminary findings from an ongoing longitudinal study of faculty writer development. Participants were recruited from three research intensive institutions, where most were initially tenure track and participating in writing groups. They agreed to be interviewed annually for up to six years to share their practices, needs, and experiences as writers. Rather than focus on these writers' daily habits—a focus I argue too easily excludes writers whose developmental trajectories do not fit the mold—I take a holistic approach that investigates how faculty experience and story (Clandinin) their writing lives and explore how that understanding might counter the "pervasive behaviorist narrative" of faculty writer development (Johnson 67).

More specifically, I draw on the concept of self-authorship from the field of human development to reveal epistemological, intrapersonal, and interpersonal dimensions of development, typically unaccounted for in faculty writer support efforts. While writing consultants offer conceptual knowledge—rhetorical considerations of audience or strategies for writing cohesive paragraphs—and popular scholarship abounds with behavioral recommendations based on the best practices of successful writers, these types of support are rarely considered in relation to broader aspects of human development. By using self-authorship as a framework for interpreting stories shared by faculty writers, I show how struggles with meaning making, shifting relationships and identity negotiation are, indeed, entangled in writing lives and must be addressed as part of a holistic approach to faculty writer support.

This line of research is relevant for composition studies because we all work with faculty writers. Some of us hold official positions as writing consultants or faculty developers, others work with writers as journal editors and reviewers, advisors, peer mentors, department chairs, and tenure and promotion committee members. Moreover, many of us are faculty writers ourselves, whether publishing in high pressure, research intensive institutions or forging time for writing in teaching focused positions. Mining stories like the ones I spotlight here—and highlighting the developmental dimensions they reveal—can reorient us to the work we do as and with faculty writers in a range of capacities.

Resisting the Path to Productivity: From "Tales of Learning" to "Trajectories of Becoming"

No matter the roles we play, I argue that we in composition studies should be "answerable" to the writers we impact in two ways: first, by acknowledging the political and ethical implications of our work; and second, by examining how our approaches determine access to knowledge production by facilitating the developmental trajectories of some more than others (Patel). Recent scholarship makes initial strides toward these ends. Anne Geller and Michele Eodice's foundational collection *Working with Faculty Writers*, for example, describes efforts to disrupt the myopic pursuit of peak productivity by considering faculty needs more holistically. Contributors "delv[e] into who faculty writers are, and who they might be, and conside[r] the theoretical, philosophical, and pedagogical approaches to faculty writing support" (Geller 9–10). The collection marks a new frontier in writing across the curriculum, but "the research is mostly in the 'This is how we do it here' phase" highlighting the need for more intense scholarly inquiry in the area (Hedengren 165). In that vein, researchers from across disciplines have begun to "turn the microscope inward" and systematically study faculty writers, identifying successful writers' strategies and habits of mind (Hedengren 165; Ezer; Sword). Researchers in composition studies, too, have contributed to this vital body of work focusing on the best practices of writers in our field (Tulley; Wells and Soderland).

Although the goal may be to improve access to scholarly publication by demystifying success strategies, research focused on how productive writers write stands to reinforce what Paul Prior calls "tales of learning"—linear views of development that suggest acquiring the "right" strategies will add up to a successful writing life. Tales of learning delineate particular "space[s] of knowledge and discourse" through which individuals must move "step-by-step along a sequentially graded curricular path" often "defined by the contemporary sociocultural organization of schooling." In the case of faculty writers, dominant tales of learning include stories about how successful writers navigate "space[s] of knowledge and discourse" defined by boundaries of disciplines and institutions in order to progress "along a sequentially graded path" to tenure. Tales of learning become entrenched in academic discourses, systems, and structures that honor certain developmental pathways and exclude others.

Alternatively, Prior offers "trajectories of becoming"—a story of development that "sees learning as embodied, dispersed, mediated, laminated, and deeply dialogic" taking place across multiple domains and moments of life. Prior's approach acknowledges that "emerging identity and emerging affective orientations lead learning." This vision allows that writer development does not happen linearly or in isolation but in relation to broader life-course development (Bazerman et al.; Brandt) and self-evolution (Kegan, *The Evolving Self*; *In Over Our Heads*). Therefore, those of us who work with faculty writers (in a range of capacities) must honor and promote trajectories of becoming tied to actual bodies, histories, emotional landscapes, emerging identities and lived realities.

Self-Authorship and Faculty Writers' Trajectories of Becoming

I propose the concept of self-authorship as one tool for revealing hidden dimensions of faculty writer development. First formulated by Robert Kegan (*The Evolving Self*; *In Over Our Heads*) as part of his constructive-developmental theory of self-evolution and extended by Marcia B. Baxter Magolda (*Making Their Own Way*; "Evolution"; "Three Elements"; Baxter Magolda et al.) self-authorship refers to a phase of human development "characterized by internally generating and coordinating one's beliefs, values and internal loyalties, rather than depending on external values, beliefs, and interpersonal loyalties" (Boes et al. 4). Self-authorship is both an evolutionary process and a dynamic explanatory construct that involves the integration of three developmental dimensions: epistemological (meaning making); interpersonal (relationships with others); intrapersonal (identity or sense of self) (Baxter Magolda "The Interweaving"; Werder). Education and human development researchers use the framework to understand forces (personal and contextual) shaping how young people come to "take internal and external responsibility for their thinking, feeling, and acting" (Boes et al. 4).

Although the construct may seem inappropriate for faculty who have presumably achieved self-authorship over their lives, Carmen Werder suggests the transitions faculty experience as writers and researchers "could very well entail a new professional and personal crossroad where faculty look to reconstruct their beliefs about knowledge, themselves, and their relationship to others" (283). Faculty developers, Werder urges, might do well to consider comments about "unbearable pressure" and the "'soul crunching' experience" of writing on the tenure track "not simply as passing moments of stress but as places of deep discontent, where faculty are working toward self-definition" (282-283). With Werder, I see the potential of using self-authorship as a "plausible tool" (Torres 70) for mining previously hidden dimensions of faculty writer development as well as for enacting answerable research that "articulate[s] explicitly" how it "speaks to, with, and against particular entities," including dominant narratives of scholarly success and development (Patel 73).[2]

In that vein, I use the integrated dimensions of self-authorship as a lens for uncovering aspects of faculty writers' trajectories of becoming as they emerge in interview data collected as part of my longitudinal study of faculty writer development. Interviews are semi-structured and modeled after the Subject-Object Interview (SOI) (Lahey et al.) based on Kegan's theory of self-evolution. The SOI is designed to: access individuals' ways of organizing their experience, identify shifts from one meaning-making structure to another, and trace journeys toward self-authorship. In the purest sense, SOI requires a highly trained interviewer with expertise in sociocognitive development and the ability to rigorously "score" transcripts (Lahey et al.). However, I have adapted the method to learn how faculty experience and make sense of their writing lives and explore if (and how) dimensions of self-authorship manifest in their trajectories of becoming. SOI is ideal for my purposes because it respects the many domains of life as porous rather than siloed and foregrounds the place of emotion in writer/human development.

Rather than apply the dimensions of self-authorship as a coding scheme, I use them to mine interview transcripts generated by the SOI for ways epistemological, interpersonal, and intrapersonal conflicts or transformations shape faculty writers' trajectories of becoming. For the purposes of this article, I focus on three faculty members—Sadie, Willa, and Mandy—all women in their thirties, all originally pre-tenure, and all from the same institution bearing the "very high research" Carnegie designation (*About*).[3] Twenty-five faculty writers are currently active in the study. Of these, 20 are women and five men; 19 identified as white and 6 as non-white or chose not to identify. They come from a range of disciplines including modern languages, education, architecture, social work, history, anthropology, health and exercise science, geography and environmental sustainability, though most are from disciplines in arts and humanities or social sciences. I chose these three women in part because they had been in the study long enough to complete three interviews, offering a robust picture of their experiences over two years.[4] Their experiences illustrate how scholarly writing is enmeshed in larger trajectories of becoming and how a narrow focus on increasing productivity based on dominant tales of learning does a disservice to faculty struggling to forge meaningful writing lives.

Epistemological Dimension: "I lost the ability to theorize like a poor Black girl …"

The epistemological dimension of the journey to self-authorship deals with meaning making; thus, individuals consider: How do I come to know? How do I decide what to believe? How do beliefs about knowledge influence my thinking and reasoning? For Sadie, the epistemological dimension of becoming a faculty writer involved a profound sense of loss as the ways of knowing and making meaning in her life and in her field were slowly stripped away. Sadie is now a tenured professor in education, although at the time of our first interview she was still on the tenure track. She identifies as a Black woman and describes her research as bearing witness and enacting pedagogy for Black women scholars. The following excerpt from our first interview is an origin story of sorts. She describes how the public education system failed her and how the strong Black women in her history affirmed her ability and worth through "celebrations of everyday brilliance":

> When I was in the second grade . . . I couldn't read and . . . I had a white female teacher and . . . she just refused to work with me . . . told my aunt "I can't teach her, she can't read." And my aunt . . . had me moved to Ms. J., [a] young new Black woman's classroom and within two weeks I was reading the Encyclopedia . . . [My aunt] was in the bathroom and she heard me reading aloud and she poked her head out—now she is butt-naked just remember that . . . so she walked out . . . and . . . she danced around the house and she was like 'Oh Hallelujah thank you Jesus!' She did all this. It was crazy. It was wonderful. But I was in the second grade, I was 7 years old and my aunt danced around the house stark naked for me because . . . I am about to cry . . . because I was reading . . . talk about celebration of everyday brilliance. [I]t left an indelible mark on me. It affirmed to me that I was a smart little Black girl . . . So I do sometimes internalize not-good-enoughness. I also have this really loud voice in my head that says "no the institution just wants to kill you" . . . The women in my history in my past have given that voice a megaphone.

Here Sadie alludes to a perpetual trauma she experiences as a faculty writer—she must counter her tendency to internalize "not-good-enoughness" with the reality that "the institution just wants to kill you." At the same time, she describes a deep source of strength she relies on to survive despite the suffering. Emotion is deeply rooted in Sadie's developmental trajectory; she tears up telling me about the voices of the women who celebrate her brilliance and bolster her resiliency.

This story from Sadie's past contextualizes her struggle for self-authorship as she fights to sustain internal epistemological frameworks. She explained it to me this way:

> I lost the ability to theorize like a poor Black girl from South Louisiana. I felt like when I first became a [doctoral] student . . . there were insights that I used to have that were strong and clear and analyses about the academic institution that was so profound and rich and they were primarily, they were before I was introduced to theoretical frames and all these other ways of analyses. My experience growing up in South Louisiana was the theoretical frame and the analytical tool that I used to think about the institution. And the longer I have been here the less able I am to draw on those frames . . . They should call . . . the theoretical frame an enslaver."

Here, Sadie eloquently describes her epistemological enslavement. Her experience as a "poor Black girl" shapes her approach to knowledge construction as means of challenging corrupt institutions that have chronically failed to serve her and acknowledge her worth. Yet, the longer she is part of the institution, the more she loses access to her way of theorizing. She recognizes the loss as a form of systemic oppression related to race, class, and gender, but is unable to reverse or slow it. Coming to terms with the loss and finding new validated frames from which to write is an integral part of Sadie's developmental trajectory, though not one acknowledged by traditional writing support initiatives that focus on "productive" writing habits.

In the same interview, Sadie explained how struggling to sustain her internally validated epistemological frameworks in the face of institutional forces that dismiss and devalue them impacted her writing life and ability to be productive.

> And then when I became a faculty member and I experienced the real academy I was like "oh, you think that I am an idiot, the rest of all you people—the rest of the world thinks I am a stupid idiot, oh!" And so that goes back to the anger part is that these constant onslaughts of undermining the value of who I am as a scholar creates a space where I get very anxious about my writing, I get very fearful about whether or not I will make it and then you know the tenure track is so elusive and whatever that it's just so . . . it's traumatizing in and of itself and I just . . . there is so much at stake . . . .

Sadie's struggle with standards of meaning making is connected to her sense of self as a writer and a human being. Because her scholarship is entwined with her sense of self, the violence of intellectual degradation becomes dehumanizing, a form of what Miranda Fricker calls epistemic injustice, "a wrong done to someone specifically in their capacity as a knower" (1). By treating Sadie as a "stupid idiot," refusing to validate her lived experience as a "poor Black girl from Louisiana," and insisting on established theoretical frameworks rooted in Western epistemologies, the "real academy" enslaves her, committing violence against Sadie as an intellectual and a human being.

Fricker describes the "harm one incurs in being wronged in this way" in developmental terms: "Where [the harm] goes deep, it can cramp self-development," she explains, "so that a person may be, quite literally, prevented from becoming who they are" (5). Sadie's story throws into relief how scholars of color and faculty from marginalized populations face disproportionate challenges as writers and humans fighting to survive systems that not only fail to recognize and support their unique trajectories of becoming, trajectories built around epistemologies of lived experience, but inflict harm on those who contort their trajectories (and epistemologies) to fit traditional "tales of learning" and pathways to success. At the same time, Sadie's trajectory reveals sources of strength for resisting dehumanization and epistemic injustice that are rarely acknowledged or fostered through traditional support efforts.

Interpersonal Dimension: "It's like writing, but other things too."

The interpersonal dimension of self-authorship is about self-in-relation-to-others; therefore, individuals ask: What relationships do I want? What happens when my needs and expectations conflict with other others? During our interviews, Willa described how shifting relationships with others, those directly related to her career in academia and those seemingly less so, impacted her writing life. For her, making progress on her book was not only "about writing," but about "other things too." Willa is a tenure-track faculty member in modern languages, literature and linguistics who identifies as a white woman. Over the last several years she's been working on the book required for tenure in her department. During our first interview in spring 2016, Willa reflected on her struggle to make progress with the book.

> I was married to a guy from Mexico City, and it ended in a very bad, violent way . . . and I wrote the dissertation there. And so there is all of these emotions wrapped up there. I saw these plays [topic of her book] there. I saw lot of them with him . . . I had this huge epiphany a few weeks ago of if I finish this book, that version of me is done. I am not a student anymore. I am not—I don't live in Mexico anymore. [T]he marriage thing and hardly anyone even knows those things about me here, so it's all gone. And so it was weird because I think it was a positive thing though it was hard. I like thinking it through, "Oh my gosh. This is why I am not wanting to just send this off and be done with it." But then I have recently gotten excited about a new project and I think, okay even if you leave things behind, you are still you and you keep doing things. It is not just an end with no beginning or no continuity. So that has been huge, it's like writing but also other things too.

Willa's reflection illustrates how her writing challenges are wrapped up in a complex trajectory of becoming that includes interpersonal relationships outside of writing. She mentions relational changes (concerning place and marital status, for example) that continue to affect her sense of self and her relationship with writing even though they are in the past. Her emotions are complicated; she experienced trauma related to a violent marriage, but at the same time she didn't want to let go of the person she was in Mexico by finishing her book. It is not difficult to imagine how behavioral strategies (such as writing fifteen minutes a day) might help Willa produce writing without meaningfully supporting her in wrestling with complex relational challenges as she strives to self-author sustainable writing practices rooted in a coherent yet flexible identity.

Shifting relationships were a central part of Willa's trajectory of becoming. In one sense, her past relationships with people and places impacted her relationship with her writing. In another sense, as her relationship with her writing evolved so did her relationship with those positioned to validate her work. In the interview excerpt below, Willa describes shifting perceptions of herself and her work in relation to journal editors and reviewers. She used to take an instrumental approach to writing and publishing, eager to satisfy tenure expectations. However, after four years on the tenure track and receipt of a contract for the book required for tenure, Willa became more invested in her writing for its own sake rather than only as a vehicle for career advancement.

> [N]ow when I'm submitting things I expect . . . at least changes . . . in a way I'm more invested in what I'm writing because it's less pragmatic . . . It's less instrumental and more invested in it but at the same time maybe because I believe in it . . . I know this is good, what do they have to say and then I can decide if I agree or not, what I need to do. Or if I need to place it elsewhere. It's more like it's my essay and I'm not just like please "What do I need to do to make this happen?" . . . I wrote to the editor of [a major journal in field] . . . and it was so funny because I really felt like okay, I'm writing to a real person and I really want to know the answers to these questions, it wasn't . . . because the 12 week article book [Belcher, 2009] told me to write a query, I'm writing a query. This is actually important to me and so it was more . . . of a relationship and I'm more of an adult probably coming across as like a mature person. For [the notecard] "angry" I have "lingering over first review, first round reviews." But I think I'm getting better.

Willa explains how her increased investment in her scholarship changed the experience of submitting work for review. Whereas she used to feel at the mercy of reviewers, she now feels empowered to make decisions about if, where, and how her writing is published. Her work was beginning to mean something more to her. Willa's connection to material from her first project was complicated because of the circumstances defining that time in her life. It was her "job keeping book" whereas she considers the new project her "real book." Understanding this trajectory and how life impacts writers' relationships to their projects and their sense of empowerment in the writing and publishing process can inform more holistic theories of faculty writer development and more comprehensive support efforts.

Intrapersonal Dimension: "You're a fucking professor ... and yet you're a fucking mess."

Whereas the epistemological dimension of self-authorship deals with meaning making structures and the interpersonal dimension concerns self-in-relation-to-others, the intrapersonal dimension deals with internal sense of self; thus, individuals ponder: Who am I? How do/should others' perceptions shape my self-perception? Mandy's stories about her writing life illustrate the significance of intrapersonal challenges and transformations. Mandy is a tenure-track professor in social work who identifies as a white woman. She had only been at the university for a year at the time of our first interview and was working to establish a reasonable pace and process for writing and conducting qualitative research. In our most recent interview in spring 2018, Mandy explained how her mental health struggles, what she calls "crazy person days," intersect with her efforts to build a multidimensional professional identity as a researcher, writer, social worker, and activist.

> So I judge myself less for having those [crazy person] days and I think about what my wife has said over the years, she's seen me go through this a lot and things that used to devastate me for weeks then moved to days and days moved to hours, so over a span of 12 years it's gotten better but it's also a struggle. I also get worse at it, because that's the nature of mental health struggles ... So yesterday I just was having a complete breakdown sobbing and I decided to go to the doctor and I now have tools to help me like Xanax and I have a therapy appointment and a psychiatrist appointment and this is more related to mental health stigma and lots of other things but basically it feels like a defeat to have to go back to those things but it's not, it's just getting treatment for an illness but I also am hard on myself and say "oh well, you're a fucking professor, you teach therapists how to be fucking therapists and yet you're a fucking mess."

As Mandy's comments show, she is in the process of making sense of her struggles with mental health, still working out the story she wants to tell herself about her most recent breakdown and her decision to seek professional help. "Crazy person days" are part of the fabric of her life, and her wife is clearly an important voice shaping the story of this life experience. Still, the series of "buts" in this excerpt highlight Mandy's internal turmoil: it has gotten better *but* it is still a struggle; the decision to seek help and tools was the right one *but* it also feels like a defeat *but* it is not a defeat. Mandy juxtaposes what she knows about mental health as a social worker and a professor who trains therapists with the reality of what it feels like to live with mental health challenges. Mandy's experience with the intrapersonal dimension of self-authorship reveals limitations of behavioral approaches to writing support based on the best practices of successful writers. The common advice to simply write more and feel less might not only fail to meaningfully sponsor but actually impede Mandy's trajectory of becoming by forcing her to compare her rocky path with the seemingly smooth paths of her successful colleagues.

Implicit expectations about how to succeed in her department exacerbate Mandy's struggle to sustain confidence and self-motivation. Her experiences exemplify the difficulty of claiming self-authorship in the intrapersonal domain, as her efforts to establish a writer identity invoke larger questions about how to "play the game" of academia while staying true to her ideals:

> I think that's what makes me feel like a fraud. I think that's imposter syndrome you know in a nutshell is oh shit, look at all these other people succeeding. They're succeeding in the right ways and maybe even if I'm succeeding, if it's not in the right way then it doesn't matter. That's frustrating . . . So if I refuse to play the game, then that's a strike against me . . . [T]here's this tension in trying to figure out how to be true to my ideals but also be realistic about wanting to keep my job.

Mandy struggles to align who she is and who she wants to be as a scholar with definitions of success that do not always feel true to her. She knows there is a "game" she must learn to play and consequences for refusing or failing. At the same time, much like Sadie, she feels she must give up her commitments—her personal vision of success—in order to succeed. That disconnect makes her feel like a fraud as she sees others around her succeed in the "right way" even as she continues to struggle. A growing body of scholarship and personal testimony acknowledges the existence and effects of impostor syndrome on academics, especially women and faculty of color (Bahn; Hutchins; Kasper; Koch; Parkman). In fact, Mandy recognizes her feelings as impostor syndrome but is unable to temper her sense of incompetence. Traditional tales of learning might treat imposter syndrome as a problematic self-perception that should be countered or ignored when it interferes with writing. Alternatively, treating imposter syndrome as a common aspect of faculty writers' trajectories of becoming inspires questions about how structures of evaluation and support actually promote damaging self-perceptions. Instead of helping

Mandy learn to play the game, acknowledging the relationship between human development and writer development might lead us to ask how we can/should change the game altogether; it might help us imagine and support pathways to success that align with faculty writers' goals and values.

The inability to see such pathways is particularly damaging for faculty whose lives are intimately bound up in their scholarship. Mandy's personal passion for her research, which focuses on LGBTQ people and religion, intensifies her struggle to stay in "the game" and be true to herself. She explained how the emotional toll of conducting research impacted her writing practice.

> [I]t's also very meticulous and very time-sucking and energy-sucking and emotional-sucking, you know, especially the research that I'm doing. I feel like it's either dreary and dragging myself through a process I'm not ready for emotionally or hyping myself up enough to be like okay, yes I really care about this, this really matters enough to be meticulous so that I can describe it [to] my readers so that I can make an impact so that I can have the right message to the right people in the right way.

Mandy's research makes demands on her time, energy, and emotional wellbeing. Compounded with her struggle to stay in the game without compromising her personal values, those demands intersect with mental health challenges she faces daily, likely impeding writing productivity. Indeed, research confirms that effects of imposter syndrome include depression, psychological distress, low self-confidence, and emotional exhaustion—all of which interfere with job wellbeing, satisfaction, and performance (Hutchins 4). That is, the emotional effort required to forge a professional path that leads to traditional academic success and resonates with her goals and values is not something Mandy can just "get over," ignore, or bracket by resolving to "write more." This brief glimpse of Mandy's developmental trajectory lends credence to Werder's notion that the unique pressures and high stakes of writing for publication might shake faculty members' abilities to self-author their writing lives.

Mandy's emotional labor demonstrates the role of intrapersonal challenges in faculty writers' ongoing development as writers, scholars, and humans, just as Willa's narrative shows how interpersonal relationships shape writers' perceptions of their writing projects and identities and Sadie's struggle to defend theoretical frames rooted in lived experience illustrates the debilitating reality of epistemological injustice. By surfacing dimensions of human development, their stories drive home the reality that theories we have for understanding and supporting faculty writers are insufficient and potentially harmful. Challenging and revising these limited understandings is urgent because how we define productivity, success, and the work of writing informs institutional policies and practices that determine access to the academic enterprise; they have immediate, lasting impact on the material lives of writers and will significantly shape the future of academia. Because we dedicate our professional lives to researching and supporting writing/writers, composition studies scholars are well positioned and, I argue, obligated to develop research-based approaches to faculty writer development that counter accepted tales of learning and account for multidimensional trajectories of becoming.

Conclusion: Advocating for Diverse Trajectories of Becoming

No matter how we work with writers—as faculty developers, peer mentors and colleagues, tenure evaluators, and/or as journal editors and reviewers—we have opportunities to support and advocate for diverse trajectories of becoming. For example, as Werder suggests, faculty developers who facilitate writing groups might take a cue from Baxter Magolda's (*Making Their Own Way*) work with college students and foster the intrapersonal dimension by inviting self-reflection on writing-related goals, identities, and relationships. Werder asks the faculty writers she mentors to create a metaphor for their writing selves. Comparing their metaphors with those of fellow writers makes faculty more aware of their unique composing processes and more forgiving when their process or "output" doesn't look like their peers'. Werder goes so far as to suggest that writing mentors use the self-authorship framework and vocabulary to help faculty focus on "sustaining a secure internal sense of self" despite dominant tales of learning and homogenized expectations for scholarly publication that urge reliance on external forces (290).

Those of us who support writers more informally as mentors and colleagues can also embrace a holistic view of writer development. Holly M. Hutchins highlights how social interactions can become "an adaptive coping strategy in helping faculty address uncertainty in their identity development, especially in forming realistic attributions concerning doubts about their professional legitimacy" (5). Intentional exchanges attuned to intrapersonal dimensions of writer development could help "normalize imposter tendencies" (5) by reinforcing the natural place of emotion in academic writing lives, including feelings such as self-doubt that are not validated in dominant discourses of success. Understanding writer development in terms of self-authorship reiterates the need for "responsive" and "transformative" mentorship based on relationality and mutuality (Hinsdale; Glenn). Long advocated by feminist and race scholars, critical mentoring challenges structures and ideologies that leave unattended the needs of so many faculty writers, especially those from marginalized groups

(Berry and Mizelle; Cooper and Stevens; Gutiérrez y Muh et al.; Ribero and Arellano; Rockquemore and Laszloffy).

We can pursue this transformative mission in our roles as tenure evaluators, journal editors, and reviewers by acknowledging the impact of the academy's long history of exclusion and the "colonial nature of our knowledge systems" on writing lives (Hinsdale 21) and dismantling problematic practices that isolate intellectual work from the bodies, histories, and relationships of writers. As Michael Day et al. point out, senior scholars have a vital role in (re) defining what appear to be neutral standards of scholarly success. Viewing writer development through the lens of self-authorship confirms that, to borrow Irwin Weiser's words, "one size clearly does not fit all" when criteria for annual evaluation and tenure review equate fairness with sameness (qtd. in Day et al. 187). Witnessing the harm caused by narrowly defined standards positions us to stand up for trajectories of becoming that do not fit the mold of particular departmental or intuitional tales of learning.

Awareness of how writers grapple with dimensions of self-authorship along diverse trajectories of becoming positions us to embrace "inclusion activism" as journal editors and reviewers who are able to identify and "willing to challenge operations that exclude and diminish the experience and knowledge of some while propping up that of others" (Blewett et al. 274-75). As a construct, self-authorship becomes a mechanism for "jam[ming] the system" for revealing how dominant tales of development and success are constructed and harmful and therefore able to be disrupted and reconceived (274). When editors value diverse trajectories and offer multidimensional support for writers, journals are more likely to become "sites that enlarge and help to grow our scholarly communities rather than follow well-worn grooves" (275).

Review practices are an important part of inclusive publishing. Journals such as *Composition Studies* (winner of the 2017 Outstanding Composition and Rhetoric Journal Award in Recognition of Inclusive Editorial Practices), *Literacy in Composition Studies*, and the new journal *Writers: Craft & Context* have made this clear with their commitments to working with authors, including those new to academic publishing, to revise and develop promising work before and after formal review. As Lars Söderlund and Jaclyn Wells point out, "now is the time" to decide what peer review should be and do in our field (119). Attention to self-authorship can ensure that a holistic view of writer development shapes our efforts to make peer review a sustaining rather than traumatic aspect of faculty writers' developmental trajectories.

Finally, composition studies researchers should include faculty writers in our efforts to develop robust theories of lifelong writing development. My use of self-authorship as a tool for mining the stories of faculty writers has offered a glimpse of just how much we do not know about their needs and experiences. The gaps in our understanding are urgent because decisions about support structures and assessment mechanisms, decisions that determine the nature of the academic enterprise and who has access to it, are too often made by those who do not have declarative and procedural knowledge of writing or research-based understanding of writer development. Our decisions about if, when, and how to focus on faculty writers are "profoundly ethical and political matters" (Prior). Furthermore, "when we ask what people need to know in order to advance inside a graded domain [in the case of faculty writers the track to tenure and promotion] instead of how people might become advanced in a life, we are likely to create obstacles rather than pathways to becoming" (Prior). On the contrary, treating development as "becoming" honors the humanity of faculty writers and calls for the transformation of dehumanizing systems, structures and policies.

Acknowledgments

I would like to thank the faculty writers who so graciously shared their experiences and perspectives as research participants. Many thanks to Christine E. Tulley and an anonymous reviewer for detailed suggestions that improved this piece. I am grateful to Shannon Madden; our collaborative work on the writing lives of emerging scholars helped me see faculty writers' stories with new eyes. Finally, I would like to thank Michele Eodice for her ongoing guidance in support of my work as well as Lesley Erin Bartlett and Jessica Rivera-Mueller for responding to early drafts of this article.

Notes

1. Belcher's second edition of *Writing Your Journal Article in Twelve Weeks* does guide readers to process their feelings about writing and includes a new chapter dedicated to invention.

2. The self-authorship framework has been critiqued for constructing a generalizable theory of development based on a predominantly White sample (Torres). However, I see the potential in using self-authorship not as a theory to impose on data but as one lens among many for interpreting data about participants' holistic development. Used in this way, the construct encourages careful "consideration of multiple dimensions and the interactions among the dimensions allow[ing] a more complete picture to emerge" (Torres 70).

3. Pseudonyms are used to protect the privacy of participants in this IRB-approved study.

4. I had no more than two interviews each for the 5 male study participants, so I chose not to focus on them here. More research is needed to explore possible gender differences in how writers experience and demonstrate dimensions of self-authorship.

Works Cited

Bahn, Kate. "Faking It: Women, Academia, and Impostor Syndrome." *Chronicle Vitae*, Chronicle of Higher Education, 27 Mar. 2014, chroniclevitae.com/news/412-faking-itwomen-academia-and-impostor-syndrome.

Baxter Magolda, Marcia B., et al., editors. *Development and Assessment of Self-Authorship: Exploring the Concept across Cultures*. Stylus, 2010.

Baxter Magolda, Marcia B. "Evolution of a Constructivist Conceptualization of Epistemological Reflection." *Educational Psychologist*, vol. 39, no.1, Winter 2004, pp. 31–42, doi: 10.1207/s15326985ep3901_4.

—. *Making Their Own Way: Narratives for Transforming Higher Education to Promote Self-Development*. Stylus, 2001.

—. "The Interweaving of Epistemological, Intrapersonal, and Interpersonal Development in the Evolution of Self-Authorship." *Development and Assessment of Self-Authorship: Exploring the Concept across Cultures*, edited by Marcia B. Baxter Magolda et al., Stylus, 2010, pp. 25–43.

—. "Three Elements of Self-Authorship." *Journal of College Student Development*, vol. 49, no. 4, July 2008, pp. 269–84, doi:10.1353/csd.0.0016.

Bazerman, Charles, et al. "Taking the Long View on Writing Development." *Research in the Teaching of English*, vol. 51, no. 3, 2017, pp. 351–60.

Belcher, Wendy Laura. *Writing Your Journal Article in 12 Weeks: A Guide to Academic Publishing Success*. SAGE, 2009.

Berry, Theodorea Regina, and Nathalie D. Mizelle, editors. *From Oppression to Grace: Women of Color and Their Dilemmas in the Academy*, Stylus, 2006.

Boes, Lisa M., et al. "Foundational Assumptions and Constructive Developmental Theory." *Development and Assessment of Self-Authorship: Exploring the Concept across Cultures*, edited by Marcia B. Baxter Magolda et al., Stylus, 2010, pp. 3-23.

Blewett, Kelly, et al. "Editing as Inclusion Activism." *College English*, vol. 81, no. 4, 2019, pp. 273–96.

Brandt, Deborah. "Writing Development and Life-Course Development: The Case of Working Adults." *The Lifespan Development of Writing*, edited by Charles Bazerman, et al., NCTE, 2018. pp. 244-71.

About Carnegie Classification. The Carnegie Classification of Institutions of Higher Education, http://carnegieclassifications.iu.edu/2010/. Accessed 1 Apr. 2020.

Clandinin, D. Jean. *Engaging in Narrative Inquiry*. Routledge, 2016, doi: 10.4324/9781315429618.

Cooper, Joanne E., and Danelle D. Stevens, editors. *Tenure in the Sacred Grove: Issues and Strategies for Women and Minority Faculty*. SUNY P, 2002.

Day, Michael, et al. "What We Really Value Redefining Scholarly Engagement in Tenure and Promotion Protocols." *CCC*, vol. 65, no. 1, 2013, pp. 185–208.

Driscoll, Dana Lynn, and Roger Powell. "States, Traits, and Dispositions: The Impact of Emotion on Writing Development and Writing Transfer Across College Courses and Beyond." *Composition Forum*, no. 34, 2016, files.eric.ed.gov/fulltext/EJ1113424.pdf.

Driscoll, Dana Lynn, and Jennifer Wells. "Beyond Knowledge and Skills: Writing Transfer and the Role of Student Dispositions." *Composition Forum*, vol. 26, 2012, compositionforum.com/issue/26/beyond-knowledge-skills.php.

Ezer, Hanna. *Sense and Sensitivity: The Identity of the Scholar-Writer in Academia*. Vol. 6, Sense Publishers, 2016, doi: 10.1007/978-94-6300-241-7.

Fricker, Miranda. *Epistemic Injustice: Power and the Ethics of Knowing*. Oxford UP, 2007, doi: 10.1093/acprof:oso/9780198237907.001.0001

Geller, Anne Ellen. "Introduction." *Working with Faculty Writers*, edited by Anne Ellen Geller and Michele Eodice, Utah State UP, 2013, pp. 1–18, doi: 10.2307/j.ctt4cgs6g.5.

Geller, Anne Ellen, and Michele Eodice, editors. *Working with Faculty Writers*. Utah State UP, 2013, doi:10.2307/j.ctt4cgs6g.

Glenn, Cheryl. *Rhetorical Feminism and This Thing Called Hope*. Southern Illinois UP, 2018.

Gross, Daniel M., and Jonathan Alexander. "Frameworks for Failure." *Pedagogy*, vol. 16, no. 2, 2016, pp. 273–95, doi: 10.1215/15314200-3435884.

Gutiérrez y Muhs, Gabriella, et al., editors. *Presumed Incompetent: The Intersections of Race and Class for Women in Academia*. University Press of Colorado, 2012.

Hedengren, Mary. "Review of *Working with Faculty Writers*." *The WAC Journal*, vol. 27, 2016, wac.colostate.edu/journal/vol27/hedengren.pdf.

Hinsdale, Mary Jo. *Mutuality, Mystery, and Mentorship in Higher Education*. Sense Publishers, 2015.

Hutchins, Holly M. "Outing the Imposter: A Study Exploring Imposter Phenomenon among Higher Education Faculty." *New Horizons in Adult Education and Human Resource Development*, vol. 27, no. 2, Apr. 2015, pp. 3–12, doi:10.1002/nha3.20098.

Johnson, Kristine. "Writing by the Book, Writing Beyond the Book." *Composition Studies*, vol. 45, no. 2, Fall 2017, pp. 55–72.

Kasper, Joseph. "An Academic with Imposter Syndrome." *Chronicle of Higher Education*, 2 Apr. 2013, chronicle.com/article/An-Academic-With-Impostor/138231.

Koch, J. "Coping with Feelings of Fraudulence." *Tenure in the Sacred Grove: Issues and Strategies for Women and Minority Faculty*, edited by Joanne E. Cooper and Danelle D. Stevens, SUNY P, 2002, pp. 107–15, doi:10.1002/ajmg.10123

Kegan, Robert. *In Over Our Heads: The Mental Demands of Modern Life*. Harvard UP, 1994.

—. *The Evolving Self: Problem and Process in Human Development*. Harvard UP, 1982.

Lahey, Lisa, et al. *A Guide to the Subject-Object Interview: Its Administration and Interpretation*. Minds at Work, 2011.

McLeod, Susan H. "Some Thoughts about Feelings: The Affective Domain and the Writing Process." *CCC*, vol. 38, no. 4, 1987, pp. 426–35, doi:10.2307/357635.

Parkman, A. "The Imposter Phenomenon in Higher Education: Incidence and Impact." *Journal of Higher Education Theory and Practice*, vol. 16, no. 1, 2016, pp. 51–60, doi: 10.1111/hea.12061_11

Patel, Leigh. *Decolonizing Educational Research: From Ownership to Answerability*. Routledge, 2015, doi: 10.4324/9781315658551.

Prior, Paul. "How Do Moments Add Up to Lives: Trajectories of Semiotic Becoming vs. Tales of School Learning in Four Modes." *Making Future Matters*, edited by Rick Wysocki and Mary P. Sheridan, Computers and Composition Digital Press/Utah State UP, 2018, ccdigitalpress.org/makingfuturematters.

Ribero, Ana Milena and Sonia C. Arellano. "Advocating Comadrismo: A Feminist Mentoring Approach for Latinas in Rhetoric and Composition." *Peitho Journal*, vol. 21, no. 2, 2019, pp. 334–56.

Rockquemore, Kerry A. and Tracey A. Laszloffy. *The Black Academic's Guide to Winning Tenure—Without Losing Your Soul*. Boulder, Lynne Rienner Publishers, 2008.

Silvia, Paul J. *How to Write a Lot: A Practical Guide to Productive Academic Writing*. American Psychological Association, 2007.

Söderlund, Lars, and Jaclyn Wells. "A Study of the Practices and Responsibilities of Scholarly Peer Review in Rhetoric and Composition." *CCC*, vol. 71, no. 1, 2019, pp. 117–44.

Stenberg, Shari J. *Repurposing Composition: Feminist Interventions for a Neoliberal Age*. Utah State UP, 2015, doi: 10.7330/9781607323884.

Sword, Helen. *Air & Light & Time & Space: How Successful Academics Write*. Harvard UP, 2017, doi: 10.4159/9780674977617.

Torres, Vasti. "Investigating Latino Ethnic Identity within the Self-Authorship Framework." *Development and Assessment of Self-Authorship: Exploring the Concept across Cultures*, edited by Marcia B. Baxter Magolda et al., Stylus, 2010, pp. 69–84.

Tulley, Christine E. *How Writing Faculty Write: Strategies for Process, Product, and Productivity*. Utah State UP, 2018, doi: 10.7330/9781607326625.

Wells, Jaclyn M., and Lars Söderlund. "Preparing Graduate Students for Academic Publishing: Results from a Study of Published Rhetoric and Composition Scholars." *Pedagogy: Critical Approaches to Teaching Literature, Language, Composition, and Culture*, vol. 18, no. 1, 2018, pp. 131–56, doi:10.1215/15314200-4216994.

Werder, Carmen. "The Promise of Self-Authorship as an Integrative Framework for Supporting Faculty Writers." *Working with Faculty Writers*, edited by Anne Ellen Geller and Michele Eodice, Utah State UP, 2013, pp. 279–93, doi: 10.2307/j.ctt4cgs6g.21.

Career Killer Survival Kit: Centering Single Mom Perspectives in Composition and Rhetoric

Alex Hanson

This article argues for greater attention to the embodied experiences and material practices of single mothers in the academy. Using critical imagination (Royster and Kirsch) to analyze how texts in the field have represented single motherhood, I identify three patterns of how mothers complete work, or what I term survivalist strategies to resist career killing. Considering these strategies result from an absence of institutional support systems and structures, I also provide suggestions and resources for better supporting single moms in academia.

A semester into my PhD program, I began the process of divorce and found myself learning how to single parent. Such a transition made me more aware of the absences of support for graduate student parents in general, and single parents in particular. I also became more aware of how the challenges and experiences of a single parent can get lost in the challenges and experiences of parents more generally. I recognized the conflation of parenting identities and how various identities get erased in that conflation. And I realized that my parenting experience presented challenges I had not seen reflected in the work I read on academic motherhood. Specifically, I learned how important a support network is as a single academic parent. I first realized this through experience. I could no longer count on getting any work done after my daughter went to bed because when she woke up, I was her only means of support. The weekends, at one time spaces of potential with open, uninterrupted work time, quickly disappeared, as I became the primary parent. Conference options became more complicated without a consistent source of care. Supplemental job opportunities that required working on nights and weekends were no longer opportunities. I learned how to maximize 15-minute intervals to write, compose emails asking for extensions and reschedules of meetings, explain class cancellations due to a sick child, and maneuver an uphill campus with a stroller and a 2 ½ year old when she couldn't go to daycare.

My experience led me to do what I think most academics do in moments of uncertainty—research. I read about mothers and mothering experiences in academia, and in this reading, I encountered the term "career killer,"[1]: from Mary Ann Mason, which she uses to describe what having children means for women in academia—"For men, having children can be a slight career advantage and, for women, it is often a career killer." The use of "career killer" implies that children are a professional death sentence for women, and I recognize the subversive career killers in my own experience—the lack of uninterrupted time, the need to bring my daughter to class when she was sick, the need to cancel class when bringing her was not an option, the conference constraints due to a lack of alternative care, the inability to attend invited lectures or other departmental events because I couldn't get a babysitter. Single mothers are often working in a system with supports that are not designed for them, so how do they make a survival kit as a means of resistance to career killers? I decided to keep reading.

Reading revealed that representations of single mothers are largely absent from academic scholarship more generally and from composition and rhetoric in particular. Kate Vieira's "Fieldwork with a Five-Year-Old: A Summative Report" is an exception. In the article, Vieira describes her experience of completing fieldwork with her daughter in Latvia after her recent divorce. Through her descriptions of single motherhood, like packing a stuffed bunny and booster seat alongside a laptop, she reveals how the worlds of scholar, mother, and divorcee are enmeshed. She shares how she survives as a single mom in academia working as both a mother and teacher-scholar-writer. Vieira's representation shows the embodied experience and material practice[2] of a single mom going through a divorce. She shares the tools in her survival kit, like having a bubble popping game on her iPhone to occupy her daughter so that Vieira could conduct research interviews and countering financial challenges by taking on substantial student debt.

The notable presence of Vieira's article indicates gaps in the scholarship, which raises the question: Why is there such an absence of scholarship like Vieira's exploring how single mothers resist the career killer connotation and survive? Part of this absence may be due to single mothers' material circumstances and resources, and the constraints these place on publishing, particularly time (single moms do not have a lot of it), but part of it may also be due to the stigma connected to a single mother identity and the potential risks in being an openly single mom in academia. Single mothers who experience a "chilly climate" in higher education find various ways of dealing with the stigmatization they experience—"…they use a variety of strategies to manage their identity that include passing, using techniques of information control, and covering," but some single mothers also, "…actively challenge the stereotypes of single mothers they encounter in classrooms and across campus" (Duquaine-Watson 146). In other words, "stigma management" could be a factor in the lack of single moms' experiences in composition and rhetoric scholarship, but it also has the potential to be a tool to resist and challenge negative perceptions and stereotypes of single mothers in academia (Duquaine-Watson 156).

A single mother's identity and position shape how she lives and moves through the world. I conceive of single mothers as women who are divorced, widowed, or unmarried who single parent their children. And I understand mother as an identity to be inclusive of a range of embodied experiences including but not limited to "othermothers," (Collins 120) "geographically single mothers," (García-Louis) transgender mothers, adoptive mothers, egg-donor mothers, and gestational, or birth mothers. While single mother is the focus in this article, familial structures and experiences within those structures vary. While I do not have familiarity with the experiences of parents who may be living across states or countries while raising children, the experiences of single fathers, those who have a partner and children but choose to forego marriage, or a range of other familial structures and experiences, I do have familiarity with the marginalization of single mothers.

Single mothers may share challenges with single parents, but the stigmatization attached to single mothers means that how they combat those challenges, their career killer survivalist techniques, are unique to them. In explaining the contrast between stigmatization of single mothers compared to single fathers, Ruth Sidel writes, "Single mothers are often defined as deviants who are dangerous to their children, to the well-being of their family and of *the* family, and the wider society as a whole…single fathers are often seen as exemplary citizens, acting in ways that far exceed society's expectations of them and thereby meriting honor and respect in the community" (22-23). The experiences described and changes I advocate for may apply to single parents as a group, but single mothers are the focus as a means of resistance to their stigmatization and marginalization.

My experiences as a single mother and my research have informed my awareness of the need for a variety of support systems and structures in academia. In order to better understand what those support systems and structures might look like, there needs to be greater knowledge of experiences. We need to look at how the field has represented single motherhood and how the material conditions and embodied experiences of single mothers are rendered invisible, making it easier for these aspects to slip out of concern. An examination of how the field has represented embodied experiences and material practices of single motherhood and how single mothers have often been spoken for or about (or not at all), offers potential for developing policies, structures, and systems of support at the departmental, institutional, and organizational level. Such policies, structures, and systems can build on the survival kits single mothers, and those who work to support them, have already tried to create. In this article, I focus on and analyze scholarship that centers the lives of mothers in composition and rhetoric. In my analysis, I identify three patterns of how mothers complete work, or survivalist strategies to resist career killing—mothering strategies and tactics, informal support, and structural and institutional support. These strategies make visible how in the absence of institutional support—mothers, specifically single mothers—must develop their own support systems and strategies to survive.

Making space for the consideration of single mothers creates an opportunity to look at the kinds of supports that exclude mothering bodies and to develop a greater understanding of the range of ways women in composition are getting work, including academic, domestic, and mothering work, done; such understanding is developed by looking at "interstitial gaps" in the scholarship—"the unheard, unthought, the unspoken" (Pérez 5). In *The Decolonial Imaginary: Writing Chicanas Into History,* Emma Pérez describes how she refers to grievances filed by the women of Yucatán with the Departments of Justice and Labor from 1915-1918 (49). Pérez's reliance on these grievances to understand how women chose to speak out against injustices demonstrates the need to be resourceful when representing and understanding marginalized experiences and histories. Without being able to get a sense of these accounts from the women themselves, there is a turn to the legal documentation about these women's experiences, which includes their voices and their words, but not necessarily from their own perspective. It is a retelling of their experiences from someone else. Like Pérez, I am looking to make the silences heard and also looking to the interstitial spaces where single mother experiences surface as places for expansion and further consideration (5).

In my search to find a way to make space for consideration of single mothers in composition and rhetoric, I implement "critical imagination," which provides a means to explore the marginalization of single mothers and the implications of that marginalization. I use critical imagination to identify the gaps in existing research as a way to inform future scholarship. Such a method acts as "an inquiry tool, a mechanism for seeing the noticed and the unnoticed, rethinking what is there and not there, and speculating what could be there instead" (Royster and Kirsch 20). Critical imagination encompasses "tacking in" which allows researchers to—"… focus closely on existing resources, fragmentary and otherwise, and existing scholarship to assess what we now understand and speculate about what seems to be missing" (72). In applying critical imagination, I look at scholarship that considers the material practice and embodied experience of mothering to see what a career killer survival kit encompasses for single mothers. I tack in to gain a sense of the ways in which single mothers and support systems and structures are positioned. I analyze three articles—two from a special issue in *Composition Studies*, and one from *Writing on the Edge,* and two chapters in edited collections, one from *Stories of Mentoring: Theory and Practice*, and another from *WPAs in Transition*. These texts were selected because they are from composition and rhetoric publications and in conversation with one another citationally or conceptually. They also provide insight into the representation of single mothers' embodied experience and material practice over a 10-year period. In my analysis, I focus on how the texts' reference various types of support to better understand what these representations reveal about the kinds of support systems and structures needed for single mothers to survive in academia. Here I ask: What support systems and structures are present or absent in the way mothers work in the field, and what does this mean for single mothers?

Engaging with Motherhood in Composition and Rhetoric

I have been in composition and rhetoric in one form or another—as a student or professional—for the past 16 years. During that time, I have seen and experienced the field's investment in equity and inclusion. I have benefitted from the childcare grant offered by Conference on College Composition and Communication (CCCC). At the most recent Feminisms and Rhetorics Conference, I attended a presentation where, as I listened to the presenter's WPA experiences, I watched her child play with board books and teething toys. While this may read like progress, over 10-years ago, there was a CCCC Task Force on Child Care Initiatives that secured $6,000 in funding for on-site childcare at the conference; today, the funding for childcare support from CCCCs has been cut in half, and the task force no longer exists (Glenn W67). Nearly half of eligible candidates for the childcare grant were turned down in 2019 due to a lack of funds, and a funding request submitted to the CCCC Executive committee was not approved ("Minutes of the CCCC Feminist Caucus"). The woman who presented at Feminisms and Rhetorics while her child played was on a panel alongside one of her child's babysitters, who did her best to keep the child content as the mom spoke.

Within my own experience, I have had faculty critique my approach to networking because they hadn't thought about my obligations as a single mother, and my need to leave conferences early. When I've told faculty that I considered bringing my daughter to a conference, they responded with surprise, commenting that it wasn't something they had considered before. I have had colleagues schedule conversations about article revisions after work hours out of personal preference. This meant I was video chatting about how to revise an article conclusion while simultaneously feeding my daughter dinner and then giving her a bath. My experiences are not isolated.

At conferences, I have listened as women shared how their academic institutions prohibit children on campus because they are considered an insurance liability. I have learned of women in visiting instructor positions keeping their children secret for fear of being seen as less committed to and less serious about their jobs. I have watched women with tears in their eyes share how they returned to teaching first-year composition two weeks after they gave birth. Experiences of mothers within the field reveal that while striving for equity and inclusion, the field is still working to combat traditional ideas and values.

While motherhood in composition and rhetoric has been an increasing area of focus in the published scholarship[3], considerations of single mother's experiences in the field, their embodied experiences and material practice, remain marginalized. In 2017, Nora et al. wrote about the need for greater representation of mothers' embodied experiences and material practice: "Far more research is needed. For example, further inquiry can examine what percentage of compositionist mothers are disabled, single or married, living with a mate, LGBTQ, and so forth—exploring how each of these factors uniquely impacts a mother's journey in academia" (142). This research is still just as needed today.

Representations of Single Mothers in Composition and Rhetoric

The consideration of how mothers get work done has recently increased as evidenced most notably through the formation of The Mothers in Rhetoric and Composition NCTE SIG in 2016. There has also been an increase of conference presentations on the topic, as well as upcoming scholarship like Christine Tulley's book project tentatively titled *I Know How She Writes It: Parenting, Publication, and Professionalism in Rhetoric and Composition* and Vieira's *Fieldwork: A Memoir*. However, the consideration given to the embodied experience and material practice of single mothers is still very limited and can be found in one article, Vieira's "Fieldwork with a Five-Year-Old: A Summative Report" and one blog post, Aja Martinez's "On Our Path, Me and My Libby," which appears on a website not affiliated with comp/rhet. The scholarship on the lives of mothers often acknowledges the role of various types of support used to get work done. In my analysis of such scholarship, I identified three patterns of how mothers complete work, or survivalist strategies to resist career killing: mothering strategies and tactics, informal support, and structural and institutional support. Mothering strategies and tactics are the self-resources mothers draw on to facilitate their own work, like having a child watch a television show while the mom grades papers. Informal support refers to the networks of support mothers may turn to or have available that are not formally implemented by academic institutions or based on self-resource (Hinton-Smith 92 and 113). For example, a close friend who provides the financial support for a mom to pay for conference registration, or a mentor who helps in finding care, so the mom can attend a conference. Structural and institutional support refers to the institutional policies or practices that facilitate mother's survival, such as parental leave policies. The articles in this analysis move away from what can often happen at the policy level—an erasure of multiple identities. However, even in this attention to practice through personal narratives, there are limitations in considering differences of experiences across mothering identities. An analysis of the selected articles makes visible the representation of single mothers and the roles various supports play in their career killer resistance.

Mothers, regardless of their single or partnered status, craft survival kits through a reliance on mothering strategies and tactics. While the necessity is different for single mothers, especially those who do not have shared custody or any type of co-parenting arrangement, the strategies are often the same. Mothers, and single mothers in particular, integrate their own means of support to get work done. This might mean having crayons and coloring books for a child to use, allowing space for a child to interrupt interviews, promising a child something like "Beanie-Boos" for good behavior, or placing a young child in an octagonal play area with board books, measuring cups, and other toys to keep them occupied (Marquez 78; Vieira 24 and 25). Oftentimes, these strategies and tactics are tools that provide a limited amount of time to complete work, even as little as five minutes (Marquez 78). These moments demonstrate mothers' agentive practice in avoiding subversive career killers, but because mothering strategies and tactics only go so far, there is often a need to turn to other resources, like informal support, to complete academic work.

Informal support for mothers is found in partners, mentors, colleagues, family members, and friends. When mothers write about their own experiences, they describe informal support as a means to provide care for their children, so that they can attend departmental and faculty meetings, complete dissertation writing, conduct research, grade student papers, or any other number of tasks that might surface for someone regardless of rank or institution (Vieira; Marquez). When looking at informal support as written about from the perspective of single mothers, we see how such support is about affective needs rather than material ones. For example, it can be a friend that helps with a sick child, those moments when "…a friend makes a house call, makes her voice soft, gives us her stethoscope, and my daughter stops vomiting" or offers comfort in food and housing, giving you space to, "Sleep briefly and wake in your friends' cozy *dacha* to find *blini* with fresh jam for breakfast" (Vieira 24-25). In the absence of an official policy, it can also be departments and programs allowing children on campus to "attend guest lectures, department meetings and orientations, dissertation defenses, and social gatherings hosted by professors" (Martinez, *Counterstory: The Rhetoric and Writing of Critical Race Theory*, 66)[4]. Often, using informal support involves a trade-off: hiring a babysitter can result in exorbitant amounts of student debt (Vieira 18); alternating care with a partner can become "tag-team parenting" (Marquez 77); reallocating care responsibilities can often result in feelings of guilt (Gabor et al. 102); and bringing a child to campus can often mean turning to mothering strategies and tactics to get them through the long meetings and lectures. Dependence on informal supports creates additional work for mothers where they are coordinating and organizing their own systems to complete work: mothers are the ones who need to "arrange childcare" (Gabor et al.; Marquez 78). They are left to decide how to accommodate academia rather than the other way around.

When others write about the support they provide to mothers, they acknowledge the value and importance of such support. As Gabor et al. explain, "social support is key to women's success," and they recognize that "mentees tend to seek out mentors with similar life circumstances," which suggests not all people may be able to find this support with the same amount of ease (100). For single mothers, as well as "Mother-Scholars of Color," seeking out a mentor with similar life circumstances is difficult because of the racial and gender disparities in higher education[5] (Herándex-Johnson et al. 129). However, scholarship has centered on a means of career killer survival that balances the line between formal and informal support—mentors. Mentors are described as providing support through actions like offering advice to mothers about how to deal with childcare, how to deal with feelings of guilt when prioritizing one's career over her family, and how to reallocate childcare responsibilities to a partner in order to get work done (Gabor et al. 102). Career killer survival also occurs through instructor support. For example, Gabor et al. describe granting an incomplete to a graduate student for a class she had previously withdrawn from due to morning sickness and hospitalization for dehydration,[6] and then continuing to "work through options" with the student after the incomplete was granted (105). Similarly, Kate Pantelides describes helping develop a survival kit for a single mother by letting the student bring her daughter to class, making visible single parenthood in academic spaces, and also trying to be understanding and supportive by reaching out through email when the student ended up failing the course. In both examples, instructors, who are also mothers, offer support in the absence of institutional structures and supports.

Like other types of informal support, as well as mothering strategies and tactics, when faculty describe supporting their mother students, the onus is put on the individual to determine a solution. In the previous examples, the instructors offering support to mothers in their classes are mothers themselves (Gabor et al.; Pantelides). These instructors offer a sort of ad hoc support to students to facilitate their continuation in higher education, which raises the question: What kind of support would there be for these students without these instructors? Given that "Graduate student mothers are at a higher risk of attrition than almost any other group in American Universities" (Ellis and

Gullion 153), that students of color are especially likely to be student parents (Schumacher 1), and that many student parents are single, there are multiple intersections of identity that exist for student parents, which exacerbate the challenges they face in completing their degree. These students are building a career killer survival kit within a system (higher education) that is not designed for them, one that marginalizes them. When there is a limitation in the availability of formal supports, there is reliance on, in this case, women who are also mothers with resources to make-up for that institutional absence of support.

The absence of structural and institutional support is made visible through mothers' descriptions of their embodied experience and material practice. While some scholarship recognizes the importance of funding to complete research (Vieira 23), funding to maintain a spot in a graduate program (Gabor et al. 105), assistantships (Gabor et al. 107), and therapy for mental health (Vieira 21), the scholarship also often acknowledges the need for improvement, specifically as it relates to family leave. While the Family and Medical Leave Act (FMLA) does provide some support by offering employees up to 12-weeks of time off, this leave is unpaid, and contingent on meeting certain requirements to be eligible (such as a minimum of 1,250 hours in 12-months) Additionally, graduate students are often not covered (Cucciare et al. 53). Even though "pregnancy and maternity leaves" are essential to the retention of "smart women on the faculty" (Gabor et al. 105), even if those policies are in place, there are limitations — "Without changing structures, it is hard to alter practices so that people can legitimately take advantage of family-friendly policies. And without this, people find work structures hostile to families" (Cucciare et al. 56). Cucciare et al. reference the American Association of University Professors (AAUP) "Statement of Principles on Family Responsibilities and Academic Work," and CCCC's "Family Leave/Work Life Balance" as helpful resources in developing more supportive structures, alleviating the need for career killer survivalists to draw on their own strategies. Even so, career killer survivalists still need to have certain tools in their kit, but if they have fewer tools, as single moms often do, then they have to work harder to survive in academic systems.

As outlined in the analysis above, single mom career killer survival kits contain tools that draw on mothering strategies and tactics and informal support like self-advocacy, time management, meal prep, screen time, toys, children's books, art supplies, friends and family, bringing children to campus, reading theory aloud at bedtime, turning to administrative opportunities with course releases, taking out student loans, therapy, making children and mothering visible, and problem solving, among others. The tools in a single mother's career killer survival kit may be similar to those found in a partnered mother's survival kit, but when a single mother is living off of one income, lacks the informal support of a partner at home, and is stigmatized for being a single mother, she uses her tools differently to enhance her chances of survival.

A single mom's position shapes what she has access to in her career killer survival tool kit, and also how she uses those tools. Because single moms identify in various ways—divorced with sole/shared/partial custody, separated, single mom by choice/change/circumstance, geographically single mom, among others—and are positioned differently along race, ethnicity, socioeconomic class, sex, gender, ability, and academic rank, their survival kits and strategies are different. A single mother's identity and position shapes whether she accepts a job, or even applies for one, as she weighs the pros and cons of staying rooted with reliable, informal support or moving 2,000 miles away and leaving that reliable support network behind. In Aja Martinez's experience, this meant knowing such a decision would entail needing to do more work than if she stayed to ensure her child remains connected to the language, food, and culture of her Chicana family members ("On Our Path…"). A single mother's position shapes her experiences at conferences and invited lectures. A single mom who lives in a state with no family has to figure out what to do with her children. Oftentimes, she needs to bring them with her, but finds herself coming up against "institutional red tape" and then "jumping through hoops" to make her attendance possible (Princeton Theological Seminary 07:03-08:00). And a single mother's marginal position in academia impacts her decision to buy her child equipment for an extracurricular activity or books for her Introductory Composition class. It impacts how much she publishes and how often, especially sole-authored pieces. As seen in the analysis, these decisions may be the difference between staying enrolled in school or dropping out, putting gas in her car to drive to campus or buying food for dinner. A single mom's position influences whether or not she discloses her single mom identity, knowing that "the Western culture education system privileges, supports, and validates the experiences and bodies of white, able-bodied, middle-upper-class heterosexual males," and such disclosure, particularly for women of color, transwomen, and women with disabilities, can lead to oppressive, marginalizing, and discriminatory treatment (Téllez 80).

Developing Policy to Eradicate Career Killers

While single moms are adept at creating their own survival kits, it's exponentially more impactful for academic institutions to develop polices that alleviate the need for single moms to have such kits. In other words, institutions should make policies that work to eliminate the need for single moms to make career killer survival kits. Part of doing this means including single moms' perspectives, which come from their embodied experience, in the development of policy at the organizational, institutional, and departmental levels. In *Mothering by Degrees* Jillian Duquaine-Watson writes about what is at risk in excluding perspectives and experiences of certain identities: "When the experiences of a stigmatized group are excluded, their perspectives, experiences, and unique knowledge are both devalued and cannot inform the theoretical and practical aspects of university matters as they relate to academic and student services" (158). Recognizing the survival strategies of single mothers provides insight into the uniqueness of how single mothers resist subversive career killers. This includes what tools they can benefit from on a policy level to support their academic career survival, as Jane Juffer writes, "I do not want to dismiss the importance of policy and structural change for *all* parents, but rather to stress that in order to support different family structures—something which many academics would, in theory, advocate—it must be acknowledged that the needs of single parents differ from those of couples who can extensively rely on each other's labor and emotional support" (103). In order to develop policies and change to better support single moms, there needs to be an acknowledgment of what their experiences are in the academy, those experiences that they draw on in crafting their career killer survival kits. Such moments as Vieira's strategies and tactics for conducting research abroad or Pantelides' informal support of a single mom in her class.

As previously explored, career killer survival kits are made from the contexts single moms are situated in. For instance, my dual identity as single-parent in academia means that I do not fit the ideal worker model—someone who has "The ability to devote long hours and weekends to professional advancement, to attend conferences, to move for both short-term fellowships and jobs, and to drop everything to meet deadlines [while depending] on the work of 'marginalized caregivers,' the supportive partners behind the scenes" (Kittelstrom). I am more apt to find myself in the leaky pipeline than a tenure-track position, encouraged to err on the side of caution when revealing my parental identity, and told that I am currently in the worst situation there is—a single parent in academia (Ballif et al. 182). There needs to be a move away from the idea that children are a professional death sentence, and a move towards changing the old academic culture, "which discourages family formation at all levels but is particularly unfriendly to graduate student parenthood, and especially to women," creating a risk of "losing many of our best and brightest minds" (Mason et al. 23). As we have seen, single moms respond to the absence of institutional and structural supports, "the old academic culture," with mothering strategies and tactics and informal support. Academic cultural change can happen at the organizational, institutional, and departmental level. The recommendations that follow for changes at these levels are informed by my own experience and research, as well as the previous analysis. The suggestions on this list are by no means all encompassing, but they are a starting point. While the suggestions would be helpful to partnered parents, they are a vital necessity for single moms. Implementing them would alleviate the unique burden placed on single moms, who are creative in finding solutions to the challenges they face and skilled at developing workarounds to navigate academia—a space that was not designed for them. For a list of additional resources to consult for ways to support single parents, please see the Appendix.

Organizational Level (Conferences, Invited Lectures/Workshops)

- Provide funding for parents travelling with children and materials that designate family friendly activities in the conference city. For example, in the "Welcome" section of conference programs that describe things to do in the host city, consider emphasizing restaurants and activities that are good for people with kids, along with attractions for those who are childfree.
- Make clear how family-friendly presentation spaces are. If possible, provide images of spaces to give a sense of how easy they are to exit with an irritable child, for example, and to also give a sense of how discretely a child might be able to play on a tablet or engage in other activities.
- Make clear where lactation rooms are and ensure that they are easily accessible and available during times when attendees will be present. The Thomas R. Watson Conference, as well as Feminisms and Rhetorics Conference are helpful models because they both provide detailed information online and in printed programs about where the lactation spaces are, when they are open, and how to access them, including who to contact with questions.
- Consider providing a crafting area for children. For example, CCCC provides space for presenters to create a sparklepony, and the Feminist Caucus provides an area for attendees to create quilt squares. Conferences could consider adding crafting and activity spaces for children who have outgrown daycare but are too young to freely roam the conference city or convention center.

Institutional Level

- Provide clear parental leave policies to *all* employees; this includes faculty, staff, and graduate students.
- Have family-friendly study rooms or areas on campus (libraries can be an ideal place for this). These can be locked rooms that those with children can reserve. Such spaces might include computers with scanners, a TV with DVD player and children's videos, chil-

dren's books, as well as children's toys. Have these rooms next to family-friendly, gender inclusive bathrooms.
- Provide affordable and accessible on-site childcare. While some colleges and universities do offer this, many often have lengthy waiting lists for up to two years if not more. In this case, it's helpful to provide a list of alternative childcare options in the area that have been used by other parents on campus. Such lists can be curated based on recommendations from faculty, staff, and students, and then included on university and college websites. University of Washington, Tacoma provides a chart on their student services website that includes information about various childcare options around the area such as the location, name, contact information, and childcare type (center, home, school affiliated).
- Have a Parental Resource Center (see University of California, Berkeley, University of Pennsylvania, and Michigan State University) where parents affiliated with the university can go with questions about housing, childcare, dependent care, dependent health insurance, and other caregiving related questions. If a parental resource center is not available, create a webpage with helpful links for parents at all levels (faculty, staff, and student) to access.
- Have multiple, accessible, maintained, and well-stocked lactation rooms.

Departmental Level

- Ensure that faculty members, as well as department and program chairs are knowledgeable about resources for parents at your institution.[7] For example, in their new faculty orientation, UC Berkeley has "an extensive segment on parental policies and support systems, including day care" (Mason et al. 113). Chairs of departments and programs there also receive a special orientation where they are "furnished with a toolkit that clearly explains their responsibilities in promoting use of family-friendly programs" (Mason et al. 113).
- Develop syllabus policies that consider student parents. Such policies can make clear that parenthood will not hinder a student's progress in your class, while also outlining the support available should a parent need to bring a child to campus. Dr. Melissa Cheyney from Oregon State University has a detailed policy that considers nursing mothers, what happens when school or childcare closes unexpectedly, and what is expected of student parents should they need to bring their children to class to "cover unexpected gaps in care."

- Schedule meetings during preschool and K-12 school hours. If this is not possible, provide transcripts from the meetings and/or allow participants to video into the meetings.
- Be clear about what family-friendly means for departmental events and if possible, let parents know what to expect. At a recent dinner I attended, I was encouraged to bring my daughter, even though it was in a hotel ballroom. The woman handling the RSVPs reassured me that she would be bringing her son as well, and then let me know that the food there wasn't kid-friendly, so it would be good for me to bring some snacks. This made the experience much more enjoyable because I knew what to expect.
- Have resources in your department/program that parents can use on days their children may need to come to campus, like crayons, coloring books, Play-Doh, stickers, and games; these can also often double as resources for multimodal teaching activities. Not all single parents carry these items with them, and having them readily available would ease the weight (literally and metaphorically) that a single parent carries when their child (or children) needs to come to campus.
- Video record or live stream invited talks and events your department or program holds; make transcripts for these events available, and also make clear in the advertising for these events that such resources are available.
- If you are a parent, be open about your parental status. Post pictures in your office, talk about your children, and be clear about your constraints. For example, if you say you need to leave a meeting at 3:00 to pick-up your child, leave at 3:00. This creates a precedent for others that it is okay to articulate and maintain boundaries, which is especially helpful to graduate student and tenure-track faculty mothers who may feel pressure to hide their parental status due to stigma (Mason et al. 76).
- Be considerate of when class and teaching times are scheduled. Provide students and teachers with multiple options, allow them to articulate their constraints, and work to prioritize accommodating their needs. I have been fortunate to have a coordinator who is attentive to my schedule constraints as a result of my single mom identity, making a substantial difference in my teaching and graduate experience, but not all parents are so fortunate. At one conference presentation I recently attended, a graduate student mother of three children shared how she was asked if she wanted to give up her

assistantship because her teaching schedule was incompatible with her two-hour commute and parenting obligations.

These shifts may initially be seen as accommodations, but my hope is that they can work towards means of accessibility. An accommodation approach—where there is consideration given to the various needs single mothers might have—can help make spaces, like conferences, more inclusive and accessible. What is needed is a move from reactive measures to proactive policies. Using a case-by-case basis of accommodation puts the onus on individuals to request accommodations they would benefit from. Single mothers need opportunities to share their accommodation needs, so that academia can work towards being accessible rather than just accommodating. I see accommodations as add-ons, adjustments that are made in certain circumstances. It's important to recognize the work that many people do to support single moms, however, this often happens independently of formal policies and structures. While I do not want to dismiss the importance of honoring accommodation requests, I think having to make such requests risks perpetuating the stigmatization of those making them (e.g.-single moms). In contrast, making something accessible means it is a regular and central part of the support system.

The development of support systems for single moms will benefit more than just single moms. This is not unlike what Kimberlé Crenshaw suggests for addressing discrimination, "If [those concerned with alleviating the ills of sexism and racism] began their efforts with addressing the needs and problems of those who are most disadvantaged and with restructuring and remaking the world where necessary, then others who are singularly disadvantaged would also benefit" (167). Restructuring and remaking spaces in academia, and specifically composition and rhetoric, to encompass and account for single mother perspectives and experiences would benefit more than just single mothers. Single mothers are a stigmatized identity in various contexts, but this stigmatization risks stifling the valuable insights of women's experiences navigating countless roles. By making space for inclusion of single mothers, there is an opportunity to develop a greater understanding of the range of ways women in composition and rhetoric are surviving. To begin to develop that understanding, academia—in general and the field more specifically—needs to start centering those with marginalized identities. We might start with single mothers and account for them in a way that moves beyond an accommodation stance and toward access and inclusion.

Acknowledgments

Thanks to Jessica and Gabby Spruill for making this writing possible by caring for Livy. Thanks to reviewers, Kara Taczak and Matt Davis, and my colleagues for providing invaluable feedback on this manuscript.

Notes

1. Thank you to T Passwater for suggesting the "Career Killer Survival Kit" part of the title.
2. Material practice refers to how mothers get work done, the day-to-day activity that such work takes; embodied experience refers to how particular experiences had by certain bodies shape individual behavior and responses to situations and interactions.
3. See Lindal Buchanan's *Rhetorics of Motherhood,* Heather Brook Adams' "Rhetorics of Unwed Motherhood and Shame" in *Women's Studies in Communication,* Timothy Ballingall's "Motherhood, Time, and Wendy Davis's Ethos" in *Peitho,* Lisa Mastrangelo's "Changing Ideographs of Motherhood: Defining and Conscribing Women's Rhetorical Practices During World War I" in *Rhetoric Review,* and "Visualizing Birth Stories from the Margin…" by Shui-yin Sharon Yam in *RSQ* for example.
4. There are some colleges and universities that have policies that prohibit children in such spaces or specify how long children are allowed on campus (Zahneis).
5. According to the NCES, "of all full-time faculty in degree-granting postsecondary institutions in Fall 2016, 41 % were White males; 35% were White females; 6 % were Asian/Pacific Islander males; 4 % were Asian/Pacific Islander females; 3% were Black males, Black females, and Hispanic males; and 2 % were Hispanic females."
6. Whether or not this student is a single mom is unclear, but she is the only mother in the article who is not explicitly described as being in a partnered relationship.
7. Similar recommendations for graduate student single parents appear in the forthcoming article Hanson et al. "(Re)Producing (E)motions: Motherhood, Academic Spaces, and Neoliberal Times." *Xchanges,* vol. 15, no. 1, Spring 2020.

Appendix: Sources to Consult in Developing Family Friendliness in Higher Education

Calisi, Rebecca M., and a Working Group of Mothers in Science. "Opinion: How to Tackle the Childcare-Conference Conundrum." *Proceedings of the National Academy of Sciences of the United States of America,* vol. 115, no. 12, 2018, pp. 2845-2849.

Cheyney, Melissa. "Family Friendly Syllabi Examples." *Childcare and Family Resources,* Oregon State University, 2019, https://studentlife.oregonstate.edu/childcare/family friendly-syllabi-examples.

Cisneros, Nora, LeighAnna Hidalgo, Christine Vega, and Yvette Martínez-Vu. "Mothers of Color in Academia: Fierce Mothering Challenging Spatial Exclusion through a Chicana Feminist Praxis." *The Chicana M(other)work Anthology,* edited by Caballero et al., The University of Arizona Press, 2019, pp. 288-309.

Duquaine-Watson, Jillian M. "Appendix: Supporting Single Mothers At Colleges And Universities." *Mothering By Degrees: Single Mothers and the Pursuit of Postecondary Education*. Rutgers University Press, 2017, pp. 197-212.

"Family Study Room." *Portland State University Library,* Portland State University, 2020, https://library.pdx.edu/study-spaces-computers/family-study-room/.

Lynch, Karen D. "Gender Roles and the American Academe: A Case Study of Graduate Student Mothers." *Gender and Education*, vol. 20, no. 6, 2008, pp. 585-605.

Mason, Mary A., Nicholas H. Wolfinger, and Marc Goulden. "Toward a Better Model." *Do Babies Matter?: Gender and Family in the Ivory Tower*. Rutgers University Press, 2013, pp. 96-114.

Mercado-López, Marissa M. "How Faculty Can Help Student Parents Succeed." *Inside Higher Ed.* Inside Higher Ed. 30 November 2018. https://www.insidehighered.com/advice/2018/11/30/advice-supporting-student-parents and-other-caregivers-opinion#.XoNtPUNoobM.link

Ortego, Gilda Baeza. "Academic Library Policies: Advocating for Mothers' Research and Service Needs." *Mothers in Academia*, edited by Mari Catañeda and Kirsten Isgro, Columbia University Press, 2013, pp. 151-160.

Schumacher, Rachel. "Prepping Colleges for Parents: Strategies for Supporting Student Parent Success in Postsecondary Education." *Institute for Women's Policy Research*. 2015.

Sullivan, Beth, Ebony Reddock, Jenny Nulty, and Melissa Stek. "Helping Students with Children Graduate: Taking Your College Services to the Next Level." *University of Michigan Center for the Education of Women*. Michigan Partners Project. 2016. http://www.studentswithchildren.umich.edu.

Threlfall, Perry. "5 Ways Professors Can Help Me Stay in School (From a Single Mom)." *Council on Contemporary Families,* The Society Pages. 19 August 2015. https://thesocietypages.org/ccf/2015/08/19/how-to-help-single-parents-in-school/.

Works Cited

"2018 CCCC Childcare Grants." *College Composition and Communication,* National Council of Teachers of English, 2018, http://cccc.ncte.org/cccc/conv/childcare.

Ballif, Michelle, Diane Davis, and Roxanne Mountford. *Women's Ways of Making it in Composition*. Routledge, 2008.

Collins, Patricia Hill. *Black Feminist Thought: Knowledge, Consciousness, and the Politics of Empowerment*. Harper Collins, 1991.

"Characteristics of Postsecondary Faculty." *National Center for Education Statistics,* Institute of Education Sciences, May 2019, https://nces.ed.gov/programs/coe/indicator_csc.asp.

Clery, Sue. "Faculty Pay." *NEA Higher Education Advocate,* vol. 37, no. 1, May 2019, pp. 1-39.

Cucciare, Christine P., et al. "Mothers' Ways of Making it-Or Making do? Making (Over) Academic Lives in Rhetoric and Composition with Children." *Composition Studies*, vol. 39, no. 1, 2011, pp. 41-61.

Crenshaw, Kimberlé. "Demarginalizing the Intersection of Race and Sex: A Black Feminist Critique of Antidiscrimination Doctrine, Feminist Theory and Antiracist Politics." *University of Chicago Legal Forum,* no. 1, Article 8, 1989, pp. 139-167.

Duquaine-Watson, Jillian M. *Mothering By Degrees: Single Mothers and the Pursuit of Postsecondary Education.* Rutgers University Press, 2017.

Ellis, Erin Graybill and Jessica Smartt Gullion. "'You Must be Superwoman!' How Graduate Student Mothers Negotiate Conflicting Roles." *Teacher, Scholar, Mother: Re Envisioning Motherhood in the Academy,* edited by Anna M. Young, Lexington Books, 2015, pp. 151-165.

Gabor, Catherine, Stacia Dunn Neeley, and Carrie Shively Leverenz. "Mentor, May I Mother?" In *Stories of Mentoring: Theory and Practice,* edited by Michelle F. Eble and Lynee Lewis Gaillet. Parlor Press, 2008, pp. 98-112.

Flaherty, Colleen. "Dancing Backwards in High Heels." *Inside Higher Ed* 10 January 2018. https://www.insidehighered.com/news/2018/01/10/study-finds-female-professors experience-more-work-demands-and-special-favor.

García-Louis, Claudia. "Navigating Multiple Roles: How My HaitiCan Children Made Me a Better Scholar." *National Center for Institutional Diversity,* 2 April 2019. https://medium.com/national center-for-institutional-diversity/navigating-multiple-roles how-my-haitican-children-mademe-a-better-scholar-79a176e7a0a0.

Glenn, Cheryl. "2008 CCCC Chair's Letter." *College Composition and Communication,* vol. 60, no. 3, 2009, pp. W63-W73.

Herández-Johnson, Monica, et al. "Mothering the Academy: An Intersectional Approach to Deconstruct and Expose the Experiences of Mother-Scholars of Color in Higher Education." *The Chicana Motherwork Anthology,* edited by Cecilia Caballero et al., The University of Arizona Press, 2019, pp. 129-146.

Hinton-Smith, Tamsin. *Lone Parents' Experiences as Higher Education Students: Learning to Juggle.* Niace, 2012.

Juffer, Jane. *Single Mother: The Emergence of the Domestic Intellectual.* New York University Press, 2006.

Kirsch, Gesa E. and Royster, Jacqueline Jones. *Feminist Rhetorical Practices: New Horizons for Rhetoric, Composition, and Literacy Studies.* Southern Illinois University Press, 2012.

Kittelstrom, Amy. "The Academic-Motherhood Handicap." *The Chronicle of Higher Education,* 12 February 2010, https://www.chronicle.com/article/The-Academic-Motherhood/64073.

Marquez, Loren. "Narrating Our Lives: Retelling Mothering and Professional Work in Composition Studies." *Composition Studies,* vol. 39, no. 1, 2011, pp. 73-85.

Martinez, Aja Y. "On Our Path, Me and my Libby." *Chicana M(other)work,* 03 May 2019. https://www.chicanamotherwork.com/single-post/2019/05/03/On-Our-Path-Me-and-my Libby.

—. *Counterstory: The Rhetoric and Writing of Critical Race Theory.* Conference on College Composition and Communication/National Council of Teachers of English, 2020.

Mason, Mary Ann. "The Baby Penalty." *The Chronicle of Higher Education*, 05 August 2013, https://www.chronicle.com/article/The-Baby-Penalty/140813.

Mason, Mary A., Nicholas H. Wolfinger, and Marc Goulden. *Do Babies Matter?: Gender and Family in the Ivory Tower.* Rutgers University Press, 2013.

"Minutes of the CCCC Feminist Caucus." Conference on College Composition and Communication, 15 March 2019, Pittsburgh.

Nora, Krystia et al. "Surviving Sexism to Inspire Change: Stories and Reflections from Mothers on the Tenure Track." *Surviving Sexism in Academia: Strategies for Feminist Leadership*, edited by Kirsti Cole and Holly Hassel, Routledge, 2017, pp. 136-147.

Pantelides, Kate. "The Joys of WPAhood: Embracing Interruption in the Personal and the Professional." *WPAS in Transition,* edited by Courtney Adams Wooten, Jacob Babb, and Brian Ray, Utah University Press, 2018, pp. 1-16.

Pérez, Emma. *The Decolonial Imaginary: Writing Chicanas Into History.* Indiana University Press, 1999.

Princeton Theological Seminary. "Dr. Sonja Thomas: Feminist Ethnography and 'Studying Up' in World Christianity Studies." *Youtube.* 29 March 2019, https://www.youtube.com/watch?v=z5pQO-Q4w2U.

Schumacher, Rachel. "Prepping Colleges for Parents: Strategies for Supporting Student Parent Success in Postsecondary Education." *Institute for Women's Policy Research.* 2015.

Sidel, Ruth. *Unsung Heroines: Single Mothers and the American Dream.* University of California Press, 2006.

Vieira, Kate. "Fieldwork with a Five-Year-Old: A Summative Report." *Writing on the Edge*, vol. 28, no. 2, Spring 2018, pp. 17–27. https://issuu.com/katevieira6/docs/singlemotherhoodandliteracy.

Ward, Kelly and Lisa Wolf-Wendel. *Academic Motherhood: How Faculty Manage Work and Family.* Rutgers University Press, 2012.

Zahneis, Megan. "When Colleges Frown on Kids on Campus—or Even Ban Them" *The Chronicle of Higher Education,* 24 Jan. 2020, pp. A23.

Affirming Difference: Inhabiting the WPA Otherwise

Nathaniel Street

A unique line of WPA scholarship highlights the bodily, mental, and emotional toll of administering writing programs, which has prompted analysis of the institutional mechanisms that produce frustration in WPA work. Writing programs are comprised of a wide range of (non)human institutional forces in often incoherent and unsustainable ways, which works to alienate individual administrators from their institutionalized subject-position because it prevents WPAs from recognizing themselves as good, or even coherent, administrators. In response, I argue that this multiplicity can be affirmed as a means of experimenting with the unique dynamics it makes available, but only if the recognizability of the "good WPA" is deliberately obscured. Thus, this affirmatively oriented mode of experimentation relies on, ironically enough, a careful practice of "not knowing" what it means to be a good WPA.

Leon Coburn's 1982 "Notes of a freshman Freshman Comp director *or* Lasciate ogni Esperanza void ch' entrate"[1] may very well serve as the hyperbolic Ur-source of what I have come to call "frustration narratives." This genre of writing program administration (WPA) scholarship addresses problems related to WPA work through quasi-personal and critically-oriented narratives that are often sardonic, parodic, and/or self-deprecating. Coburn not only invokes Dante's hellish signage in his title but also characterizes his single year as the director of composition at the University of Nevada, Las Vegas as one "of frustration, anger, and defeat." He continues, "no matter how bleak the summary sounds, the day-to-day reality was much worse" (9). The six-page article proceeds as a chronological litany of everything that went wrong: lack of funding, bureaucratic logjams, scheduling nightmares, and even two pregnant secretaries. He follows his account with a brief reflection on how to survive the job: find allies and slowly wear down the (enemy) faculty in a war of attrition. While Coburn does offer the caveat that directors have a unique opportunity to significantly impact students and he does offer a few "silver linings," he goes out of his way to note that he only includes this section because his wife insisted that the original draft was too negative.

---

1. Dante's "Abandon all hope, ye who enter here."

While Coburn's account is hilariously and rather self-consciously over-the-top, it nonetheless enacts and perpetuates a commonplace vision of writing program administration. WPAs are often tasked with managing massive programs with insufficient institutional support and garner little professional legitimacy for the trouble. Even a cursory survey of WPA scholarship shows that "frustration narratives" are neither new nor rare.[2] Yet, they have gained little traction outside of explicitly WPA-centric conversations. Laura Micciche demonstrates as much by the sheer fact that, in writing to a *College English* audience in 2002 about this kind of scholarship, she needed to provide an extended introduction and a direct plea to make her case that the disappointment of WPAs is worth taking seriously by a broader audience.

Even when they are read, "frustration narratives" are often and all too quickly dismissed as a kind of subculturally sanctioned form of whining. Wendy Bishop and Gay Lynn Crossley offer a glimpse of this problematic attitude by sharing a comment made by an anonymous reviewer on an initial article submission outlining Bishop's WPA experience, an experience which resulted in her resignation. In it, the reviewer laments, "I am disturbed at how easily the authors permit themselves to present this story as another victim-narrative that you hear so often in accounts of composition, of WPAs, and even of women WPAs" (74). In addition to exposing bald sexism, the rare opportunity to see an anonymous comment like this makes a predominant bias explicit and demonstrates that this bias misses what these narratives do rhetorically: they are primarily written to provoke dialogue about frustration in WPA labor and to make that work acknowledged, engaged, and transformed. Despite these efforts, the general conditions of WPA work are either ignored or dismissed – often along gendered and racial lines.[3]

The general sense that writing program administration is undervalued and emotionally taxing has not changed much in recent years. In her 2018 WPA plenary address, Susan Miller-Cochran echoes many of the key arguments made in "frustration scholarship" over the past thirty years: writing directors are constantly pulled in multiple and competing directions that often directly pit their scholarly, ethical, and pedagogical commitments against a plurality of institutionalized expectations. Meaghan Brewer and Kristen di Gennero confirm the still-marginalized place of composition studies in general, and WPA labor more specifically, in many English departments by bringing to light the "microaggressions" that invalidate the worth of composition studies

---

2. Just to list a handful: Bloom (1992), Bishop and Crossley (1996), Smoke (1998), George (1999), McGee (2005), Craig and Perryman-Clark (2011, 2016), Malenczyk (2012), DeGenaro (2018).

3. See Holbrook and Craig and Perryman-Clark.

relative to literary studies – especially in its "service" roles. William DeGenero filters his experience as a WPA through his identification with Kurt Cobain's frustration with the music industry. It's been nearly forty years since Maxine Hairston predicted "winds of change" in 1982; and while there has certainly been quite a bit of change for the field writ large, the frustration narratives published today do not look all that different from those published ten, twenty, or thirty years ago. If anything, the disappointment they express has intensified in our increasingly corporate climate.

While frustration narratives are common, surprisingly enduring, and consistent, very little has been written about them. That is, very few scholars have addressed the genre as a genre. There are at least three articles that break this norm: Jeanne Gunner's "Ideology, Theory, and the Genre of Writing Programs," Micciche's "More than a Feeling: Disappointment and WPA Work," and Matthew Heard's "Cultivating Sensibility in Writing Program Administration." While on the surface, they seem to only share a common concern for the disappointment engendered by writing program administration (which is certainly not uncommon in WPA studies), they stand out in at least two ways. First, unlike frustration narratives, these three articles largely take the difficulty engendered by the WPA position as an empirical given in order to focus their attention on the structures that produce this marginalization and frustration. Second, Gunner, Micciche, and Heard demonstrate, in their own ways, where and how WPAs might mobilize those institutional structures that tend to produce frustration differently.

Gunner and Micciche published their work in 2002 and Heard published his in 2008. Gunner and Heard's work have barely been cited at all; and, while Micciche's article has been frequently cited, the vast majority of that scholarship extends on her theory of emotions to make an argument about some other profession (e.g. Writing Center Administration in Jackson et. al.) or dimension of rhetoric and composition (e.g., the academic job market in Sano-Franchini). No one has yet adequately engaged Micciche analysis of the structures that produce frustration in WPA labor or attended to how those structures might be remobilized. We've missed an opportunity. Micciche offers a rich account of how emotion, labor, and writing program administration intersect, while Heard and Gunner imagine powerful ways of engaging and re-mobilizing the structures that produce WPA identity and emotion. But they need to be updated and rethought; this conversation is too important to become relegated to the archives of composition studies.

In advancing this inquiry, I argue that the structural dynamics of WPA labor that tend to produce frustration can be made otherwise and even affirmed. Such affirmation would deliberately blur the boundaries that separate individual WPAs from their institutionalized subject position so as to experiment with the unique and unexpected combinations that a singular multiplicity makes available. Following a philosophical tradition that runs through Baruch Spinoza, Friedrich Nietzsche, and Gilles Deleuze, I argue that an affirmative style of inhabiting the university is inclined to cultivate a lighter, and perhaps more joyful, affective disposition toward the ever-shifting and often uncontrollable dynamics of the university. I conclude by considering an example from my time as an Assistant Director of First-Year English (FYE) as part of a massive overhaul of our state flagship university's general education requirements. Our first year writing program was tasked with implementing a new learning outcome for the teaching of information literacy in an existing first-year composition course. I turn to this example because it illuminates the dynamics that intersect, and thereby multiply, writing programs. The role I played in the overhaul allows me to uniquely highlight some of the very local opportunities our WPA had in affirming the differences that emerged during the process.

Institutional Affect-Machines

Micciche's "More than a Feeling: Disappointment and WPA Work" gives an excellent account for why frustration is such a regular feature of WPA labor. Disappointment, she argues, is produced within institutional contexts because the historical, institutional, and ideological forces that shape how writing programs are inscribed within universities are often at odds with the values and beliefs that fundamentally inform many WPAs' vision of what writing programs should be. Relying explicitly on Marx's concept of alienated labor, Micchiche argues that the relative powerlessness of WPAs to meaningfully shape the programs they direct creates an "affective dissonance" between labor and laborer. The repetition of this dissonance can lead WPAs to "become *accustomed* to, even to *expect*, disappointment," which, Micciche rightly warns, restricts their ability to make productive connections to others and radically contracts the horizons of what they deem to be possible (447; emphasis original).

What is key about Micciche's analysis is that she shows how far disappointment cuts into the WPA experience. Because "work is one of the key processes through which we develop a sense of self-worth and potentiality," the institutionalized disappointment that Micciche addresses is not simply the superficial frustration caused by the kinds of logistical blockages that pop up in any environment (437). Rather, this type of disappointment arises from a deeply set self-alienation. In other words, what "gets disappointed" in these situations is our ability to see ourselves as WPAs–or at least as good WPAs. When our most fundamental commitments to writing scholarship and instruction–commitments that likely drove us to and through graduate school–are rendered incompatible with how our writing programs are inscribed in our universities, we are put in positions where we feel like our only options are futile resistance or resignation.

In response, Micciche proposes that we broaden the dialogue and material analysis of disappointment in WPA studies to include the emotional dimension of administration in the academy more generally in an effort to improve the material conditions that produce disappointment.[4] I thoroughly support these aims. They can also be supplemented; indeed, Micciche's work sets the stage for imagining such supplements. What is particularly enabling about her scholarship is that she sketches out the complexity at work in the emotional mechanisms she analyzes. One of the most recurring claims made in frustration narratives is that the sheer number of competing demands made on writing programs tend to produce what Trudy Smoke calls the "paradox of powerless power" (93). The writing program may be officially structured into the university in one way, but it is pressed upon by a plurality of forces that shape and complicate that place, multiplying it as those demands provoke its boundaries to oscillate. The program is one thing for its director, another for its (often contingent) faculty, another for upper-level administrators, another for non-departmental faculty, and many other things for the wide range of students that pass through it. Micciche reveals that disappointment is produced by a dissonance between this multiplicity and the complex identity positions that individual WPAs bring to it.

Building on this insight, I turn to the language of "affect" to describe how disappointment not only manifests as the personal experience of individual WPAs, but also as an institutional condition of writing programs. Whereas the language of emotion is likely to draw to mind the internal experience of individual WPAs (something I by no means wish to discount), the language of affect better directs us to see those feelings as symptoms of broader and more external sets of relations (the circumstances that produce the "I feel"). Furthermore, while Micciche primarily relies on the language of emotion, "affect" speaks to her titular claim that disappointment is "more than just a feeling."[5] The way she describes disappointment as something institutionally produced within

---

4. Rebecca Jackson et al. do exactly this by taking Micciche up on her call and exploring the emotional labor of writing center directors (2016).

5. Micciche distinguishes between affect and emotion in Doing Emotion, arguing that emotion better "evokes the potential to enact and construct, name and defile, become and undo–to perform meaning and to stand as a marker for meanings that get performed" whereas affect speaks to the more general "preverbal, visceral conditions that encompass emotions and feeling" (14-15), though she acknowledges that she's not set on maintaining a rigorous distinction. My wrinkle on the affect/emotion relationship is important here only insofar as it complicates the boundaries between the individual-WPA and the WPA-position.

WPAs, and as something that folds back onto WPAs to shape their potential power, resonates with the concept of affect, at least within an intellectual tradition passing from Spinoza through Deleuze to, more recently, Brian Massumi and Erin Manning. In this tradition of thought, emotion tends to center on individuals and their feelings while affect points to a kind of pre-individual intersection of relations (both human and nonhuman). These thinkers tend to describe this pre-individual intersection of relations as a body; a body that is capable of affecting and being affected by others. What I'm suggesting is that the language of affect allows us to see writing programs as pre-individual bodies, whereas it makes less sense to talk about the emotional state of a writing program (for more on this, see Edbauer, 2009). This affect/emotion distinction is an important tool for exploring how the machinery of writing programs can be re-appropriated to produce different sets of relations and productions. In the next section, I turn to two scholars who effectively experiment with just this sort of appropriation in an attempt to turn disadvantage into advantage.

Rewiring the Machinery

Gunner, like Micciche, begins with the premise that writing programs are inextricably caught up within larger ideological discourses that "are not entirely commensurate with a given course or courses" (Gunner "Ideology" 7). Yet, she argues that despite this historical and institutional disadvantage, the sheer heterogeneity of ideological discourses that traffic through writing programs can actually be valuable.

Gunner advises WPAs to observe moments of instability in ideological discourses as they circulate through the university, noting that "moments of ideological ambivalence" may create opportunities for WPAs to tie their initiatives "to more culturally privileged and hence more powerful discourses... so that [they] might have material force" (15-16). For instance, Gunner points to a moment when she tapped into the language of "cultural diversity" that had been gaining sway at her institution. Gunner mobilized this language to disrupt the connection between writing and "correctness," which arose from discourses centered around colonial civility and individualism. The momentary power imbalance between these discourses, and the subsequent ambiguity it created, provided an opportunity for Gunner to articulate her initiative within a (temporarily) more institutionally powerful discourse.

Gunner, however, does not attend to the affective dimension of her approach, and we are left to think through how a tactical orientation to writing program administration bears on the affective machinery of the writing program. I write "tactical" (a word she does not use) because she effectively configures WPAs as astute observers of an ideological battlefield, looking for discord on which to capitalize.[6] I see at least two non-exclusive ways in which a tactical orientation could contribute to an affective disposition. The obvious upside is that Gunner, through a kind of institutional jujitsu, articulates a smart way of turning disadvantage into advantage. Simply put, increasing the program's ability to realize its will is empowering–and empowerment can lead to the kind of hopefulness that expands and diversifies the horizons of what we deem possible.

Tactical administration simultaneously fosters a kind of alienation because it relies on a presumed antagonism between the program and the non-program. While tactical agility can be quite effective, and is often necessary, it simultaneously demands a relatively clear articulation of "the sides." Thus, while this kind of alienation is quite different than the disappointment that Micciche highlights, a tactical orientation still has a way of alienating WPAs because it tends to entrench one's own ideological commitments while at the same time configuring the complex dynamics that constitute the writing program as a field of resources to harness. In short, the power of the writing program to affect and be affected by difference is diminished by a tactical orientation, even as the agency of the individual WPA increases. Both this decrease and increase are driven by the same configuration of power that articulates the writing program as a battlefield.

Similar to Gunner, Heard seeks to turn weakness into strength by showing how the traditionally disadvantaged place of the writing program actually makes it an ideal place from which to "sensibly" attune to ideological conflicts as they flow through writing programs. Heard argues that the vulnerability of the WPA position allows individual WPAs to develop a sensitivity to how institutionalized forces press upon, and thereby (re)shape, the identities of others. Such an attunement can disrupt our entrenched orientations because running into discordances between value systems carries with it the potential to "pull us out of our habitual patterns of thought and action" so as to reveal the impact they have on others (42). Heard provides a great example of this, wherein his desire to train GTAs according to his theoretical commitments worked to blind him to the needs of his students (44-45). Thus, by attuning reciprocally to the pressures that traffic through our programs, a sensible ethos can also reveal the larger ideological forces that overdetermine the value of writing and its function in our lives.

What is interesting about Heard's argument is that he shows how WPAs are uniquely suited to disrupt, nuance, and even transform their position as

---

6. I adopt "tactic" to invoke de Certeau's distinction between "strategy"–the general implementation of a plan based from a position of power–and "tactics"–countermovements within a field of power.

WPA into one that is more sensibly oriented toward others. Because sensibility is a posture rather than an identity, the institutionalized vulnerability of the WPA position serves as a means by which WPAs can continually revise and adapt their own orientation as they respond to the forces that constrain others. This sensible orientation seeks to disrupt our investment in the identity boundaries that work to alienate WPAs by actively building connections to others in ways that enlarge the scope of what counts as "us."

Yet, I do not think that it is immediately clear what kinds of affective connections are likely to be built between "us" and "other." Heard describes sensibility as "a living awareness of *outside pressures and tensions that press upon us...*" (41; emphasis added). Essentially, a sensible posture illuminates, or allows us to "witness," the local ways in which outside forces press upon others, especially the way that economic imperatives have predetermined the value of writing in ways reduce or marginalize modes of writing that do not conform to that imperative. And yet, while sensibility might jar us out of our habitual modes of being, it risks doing so by realigning the marginalized "we" against a more generally offending party (e.g. anything that we recognize as violating the identity of others). A posture of sensibility thus inclines us to code "outside pressures" as something "they" do to "us" even as the boundaries of the "they" and "us" are redrawn in response to that pressure. WPAs, for example, may come to recognize the vulnerability of other students and faculty, but only insofar as they recognize their vulnerability to a violating force–some other determinate other. So, while an ethos of sensibility is likely to redefine and enlarge the territory of a community, in founding sensibility around violence and vulnerability, Heard also creates a dividing line that shifts rather than disrupts the "us vs. them" logic.

While both Gunner and Heard open up what is possible through the WPA position, they do so in ways that do little to address the affective machinery that Micciche's work has allowed me to tease out here. This is less a critique of Gunner and Heard than it is a way of emphasizing the importance of attending to the questions and problems raised by this dimension of administration. But this analysis also raises a few questions of its own. Is there a way to administrate that is productive and yet does not, or at least is less inclined to, perpetuate alienation? Is there a way of responding to otherness without having to identify it, and thereby colonize it, according to recognizable ideologies or concepts like vulnerability and violence?

Identity, Subjectivity, and Affirmation

At this point, reexamining the dynamics at play in producing frustration and alienation provides a clearer sense of the tension operating between the "us" and "them" at the heart of this affective machinery. Each of the positions I've addressed presume a certain commitment to the individual identity of the WPA ("us") against the power of the WPA as an institutionalized subject-position always already co-opted by a host of competing claims ("them"). I want to amplify a distinction I've been making via the language of "subjectivity" and individual "identity" to tease out the significance between two networks of power. Let "subjectivity" be the complex network of institutional dynamics that constitute the WPA position that subject (or interpolate) individual WPAs to its power. Let individual "identity" be the complex network of identity positions and value commitments that both consciously and unconsciously shape individual WPAs.[7] Rendering the distinction in this way illuminates the directionality of this encounter between subjectivity and identity. Individual identity is rendered subject to the multiplicity of the WPA position, which presumes that identity is made vulnerable to the shaping power of a more dominant subjectivity. It is precisely this power differential that racializes and genders WPA bodies: the WPA subject-position, historically informed by a feminized sense of "service" and racialized sense of "civility," disciplines individual-WPAs by overdetermining their value, making it especially hard for black bodies to become WPAs at all.

Making this distinction between identity and subjectivity is another way of fleshing out an important feature of the affective machinery of writing program administration. Whereas it would be more appropriate to speak to the emotional state of an individual marked by an identity, affect better speaks to the inclination, or disposition, of a pre-individual confluence of human and non-human forces institutionalized in the form of a WPA subject-position as it encounters individual WPA identity. Thus, it is not right to say that identity is emotional while subjectivity is affective, but that affect speaks to the pre-individual body that is the conjunction of an identity and a subjectivity–an orientation that inclines a writing program to affect and be affected in ways that are irreducible to any one person. It is the dissonance between these two networks of power that cultivates the disappointment of writing program administration.

There is, of course, good reason to commit to our identities as WPAs, since the forces to which we are subject disproportionately bear on the identity positions we bring to the job. As Louis Althusser might claim, the interpolating force of the "hey, you there" may well recruit both the police officer and the subject of his hail to a juridical structure, but not with equal force. It would seem that the only options available to those marginalized by this disequilibrium are to acquiesce to these subjectifying forces, sincerely resist them, or tactically

---

7. Individual identity is itself a product of other networks of subjectivity: the difference between identity and subjectivity is relative.

and/or sensibly remobilize them into the occasionally subversive advantage (all while maintaining a more constant disadvantage). A general commitment to maintaining identity against subjectivity has a way of rendering the multiplicity of the writing program in only one of two ways: either as an obstacle or form of domination (as most frustration narratives confirm) or as raw material to re-mobilize (as Gunner and Heard show is possible).

While the WPA subject position is itself multiple, it is also singular insofar as it functions as a juncture point of intersecting dynamics. So, while its constituent parts are multiple, they connect in a singular fashion. The fact that writing programs are so difficult to render according to any one institutional perspective confirms that they are nothing more than the intersectional difference of a great diversity of forces–including the identity of the WPA who inhabits it. Given this relationship, I propose a different way of orienting ourselves to administration that deemphasizes the boundaries that separate individual WPA identity from the institutionalized WPA subject-position by experimenting with the particular ways a multiplicity of demands and identities and subject positions intersect each other to continually constitute and reconstitute the pre-individual body of the writing program. This would constitute a kind of affirmation of the singular difference that emerges as identity and subjectivity conjoin, folding WPA identity through a writing program and WPA subject position through one's identity. This mutual distribution blurs the boundaries between the "us" and "them" through a transformation born of conjunction.

It is perhaps easy to see this "affirmation" as a form of resignation: the disequilibrium between identity and subjectivity poses a very real threat to a WPA's individual identity–especially to those WPAs who are gendered and racialized into more marginalized corners of the academy. Yet, while it would be foolish to discount this disequilibrium, it is also important to see how subjectivity is fractured and how that fracture makes subjectivity susceptible to the differential force of individual identity. The multiplicity of the WPA subject position (all of those often-competing claims) also means that there can be no one position to which a WPA could become subject because WPA subjectivity is always constituted by an intersection of multiple forces.

Strictly speaking, then, there is no "thing" to which we could resign ourselves. There is only the difference that emerges from an intersection. For example, one's gender, race, sexual orientation, body (etc.) makes its own mark on the writing program and, thereby, alters its field of possibilities. Furthermore, historical and scholarly forces (such as those constituted in the body of what I've called frustration narratives) work as a part of the complex as well. Thus, rendering one's individual identity subject to the institutional position of the WPA means that its force bears upon the WPA subject position, infecting it with its difference. Far from simply resigning oneself to the subjective power of the WPA-position, an affirmative orientation would seek to activate the unique difference produced by the constellation of forces at work for the sake of transforming them. How might the force of frustration scholarship circulate through one's writing program? In considering this question from a racialized perspective, scholars as diverse as Henry Louis Gates Jr., Jeffrey Nealon, and Amber Kelsie note that such an intensification might transform questions concerning racial inclusion into experiments of black transformation. Following this line of thinking, the affirmative-WPA would become a virus that infects the institutionalized body they inhabit, working to introduce their difference into a field of asymmetrical relations.

An affirmative orientation to administration would require a different kind of commitment to the identity of the WPA: a commitment to identity as a kind of antigen that provokes a response in a larger institutional body rather than as a territory whose integrity must be protected. This perspective, though, would require that we deliberately obscure the boundaries that distinguish the constituent claims on the writing program so the differences their intersections create come to the fore and their recognizability recedes into the background. Affirmation cares about what identity can do and become more than with what identity is.

John Muckelbauer proposes a similar orientation, but as a strategy for how we read scholarship. When we read so as to identify the concepts, problems, and texts that a work mobilizes, we dramatically reduce the inventive power of how they might intersect in interesting and unforeseen ways. As Muckelbauer puts it, "experimenting with what a concept can do requires a certain uncertainty about what the concept is" (48). This kind of experimentation requires a reader to actively not-know the boundaries that separate a conceptual landscape. In the case of writing program administration, if we pretend to know, in a determinate sense, what it is to be a good WPA in advance–or even know the boundaries that separate the WPA from the non-WPA–we simultaneously work to shut down what a WPA could do other than accept, instrumentalize, resist, or acknowledge those multiple dynamics that intersect writing programs.

This "not knowing" is not ignorance. We should be immersed in administrative practice and theory as well as the historical practices that gender and racialize WPA labor. We should carefully attend to the unique organization and histories of our institutions. As a heuristic, this active not-knowing is an explicit and carefully cultivated orientation toward what the dynamics that make up writing programs are capable of doing other than solidifying and reifying a particular vision of them. In other words, it is a "not knowing in advance" what a dynamic can produce.

Consider the affective dimension of this affirmative orientation. Gilles Deleuze argues that there are two principal kinds of affects: joy and sadness

(Deleuze *Spinoza* 48-51). Sadness is the state of a body (always pre-individual multiplicities for Deleuze) decreasing its ability to affect and be affected by others. Joy is the state of a body increasing its ability to affect and be affected by others. "Sadness" could easily stand in for what Micciche calls disappointment and loneliness. Severing the connections between labor and laborer, or between an individual identity and an institutionalized subject position, decreases the ability of writing programs to affect and be affected by difference. It is important to see that the tactical and sensible orientations that Gunner and Heard propose increase the vitality of the WPA-body only insofar as that-which-is-different from the individual WPA is made a resource. Though empowering, and thereby joy-making to a degree, the boundaries these approaches reify also cut WPAs off from its inventive potential by focusing on ready-made identity claims.

An affirmative orientation to administration configures writing programs less in terms of bounded territories and more in terms of the intersecting lines that traverse through those territories; indeed, it allows us to see these territories as nothing more than by-products of a prior relationality. This allows the territorial boundaries of the writing program to recede into the background as the WPA emerges as a singular, pre-individual body: identity + subjectivity. What is joyful about affirmation is that it unites and intensifies the multiplicity of the WPA body for the sake of its own transformation. Another way of putting it: the joy of affirmation lies in the becoming of a body as it expresses itself into something new, whereas sadness lies in the calcification of the boundaries that alienates the being of that body. This is why "becoming" a WPA can never be a matter of a body realizing itself as a WPA ("to become a WPA"), but only ever refers to the continual making and unmaking process of becoming: the gerund makes "becoming" something perpetually unsettled.

Affirming a General Education Revamp?

From 2011 to 2013, I was involved as an Assistant Director of First-Year English and RA to our Director of First-Year English in a major initiative to revamp the general education program of a state flagship university system. The project was inaugurated in the form of a question, in 2005, by the university's then-provost: "What do our students need to know to thrive as well-educated citizens in the twenty-first century?" This question, which was largely informed by the 2005 study "College Learning for the New Global Century" by the *Association of American Colleges and Universities* (AACU), kicked off over a decade's worth of institutional change. Because some of these requirements necessitated that some courses serve a much larger population and, in other cases, entirely new courses had to be developed for new requirements, student demand shifted and put pressure on departments to respond. It is no exaggeration to describe this initiative as a multiple and differential force that changed name, shape, and intensity as it distributed through the university.

The new requirements are grounded in collections of learning-outcomes developed by faculty committees designated as "subject matter experts" (e.g., the Written Communication requirements (CMW) were developed by representatives from English, business, and journalism and mass communication). Thus, departments no longer "own" required courses. Theoretically, any course could fulfill the new requirements, so long as it is approved by the requisite committee. Given this interdisciplinary structure, any department that wishes to submit a course for approval would need to appeal to a committee that is primarily, or even exclusively, composed of faculty outside of their own department.

By the time I was involved in 2011, our director had already managed to have our two-semester first-year writing sequence (ENGL 101 and 102) approved to grant the six-required-credits of CMW and had the second semester course (ENGL 102) tentatively approved to grant the 3-credits needed for the new information literacy requirement (INF). This required that we "overlay" INF into ENGL 102 in ways that satisfied criteria devised by a completely non-English faculty (the "overlay" itself was a product of prior compromise on how new requirements would be made available to students, especially in the initial years after the requirements took effect). In effect, our job was to re-create ENGL 102 to satisfy CMW and INF requirements articulated and assessed by two separate, almost exclusively non-English, faculty bodies.

My relatively moderate involvement as a graduate student, and especially my position as liaison to the library, put me in a particularly good position to observe how our director responded to the pressures put on the program as well as some of the multiple ways in which the initiative circulated through the university. This allows me to highlight how Micciche, Gunner, and Heard's scholarship sheds light on those approaches as well as how and where an affirmative approach to administration was made available.

There is a relatively straightforward way of telling this story that highlights the emotional machinery at work that Micciche makes visible. The general education revamp was created by powers far beyond our director's control. The ideological commitments that shaped the CMW and INF requirements did not entirely align with hers, yet they pressed upon the program nonetheless. She did her best to shape the requirements upstream, as they passed through exploratory committees and task forces. She negotiated with other faculty from the library and the schools of business and of journalism and mass communication, who served on the development committees, (e.g., limiting emphasis on grammatical correctness). On the other side of the power divide, she did her best to involve and facilitate administrators and instructors affected by the change across the university's regional two-year campuses.

Some of these negotiations went well; others were more fraught. For example, her efforts to lower the enrollment cap on ENGL 102 to accommodate the added grading and prep time that INF demands of faculty did not succeed. Ultimately, most of the emotional weight fell on her shoulders as she attempted to balance her duty to shape, resist, implement, and distribute the new learning outcomes.

Yet, our director's precarious position also afforded her certain tactical advantages, made more visible by Gunner's scholarship. She was able to tap into language circulating around the initiative by espousing the value of civically and globally-minded education in order to highlight the value of rhetoric's historical commitments to public engagement and of critical engagement with cultural contexts. Highlighting the dimensions of rhetoric germane to the discourse of the general education revamp, our director was also able to harness the force of the learning outcomes without having to explicitly resist them.

Counter to Gunner, Heard's ethic of sensibility emphasizes the ways in which the general education initiative rippled throughout the university, putting other departments and programs in similarly vulnerable positions, thereby highlighting how those differences might productively pull our director out of her habitual modes of seeing her administrative role. In this case, it became apparent that the university's library was put in a precarious position insofar as it marked a kind of ground-zero for information literacy expertise but had a very shallow pool of instructors and no curricular resources to speak of. Our director made me FYE's liaison to the library and tasked me with collaborating with a small group of staff who served as consultants to the INF overlay project. The work that we did not only allowed us to better ground INF instruction in information science, but strengthened the institutional ties between the English department and the library and between the library and the INF requirement, which also served to jump-start the library's own initiatives to create a new online course that also fulfilled the INF requirement. Thus, the disruptive force of the initiative created an opportunity to remake FYE's relationship to the library.

All three of these perspectives reveal important ongoing dynamics operative during our involvement in this revamp. To supplement these perspectives, I want to highlight some opportunities we had to affirm the unique difference that marked the program as a site of intersecting dynamics (e.g., between the INF and CMW mandates; between the library and FYE program; between the holistic commitments of our director and the ends-oriented values that informed the general education initiative; between the old version of ENGL 102 and the disciplinary knowledge driving information literacy instruction). Doing this, though, presumes a certain willingness and practiced artistry on our director's part to not know what ENGL 102 ought to be; or, at minimum, it required an ability to loosen her grip on that knowledge.

My research on how peer-institutions have handled combining writing and information literacy instruction in the past brought up an interesting "portfolio" model from Oregon State (Deitering and Jameson). Conversations with our library consultants had already made it very clear that worthwhile information literacy instruction needs to be recursively integrated into practice. This meant that we could not simply devote class periods to teach abstract principles of research. Furthermore, a portfolio model roughly fit with the course's pedagogical commitments and gave us a path forward for synthesizing writing and research instruction. But the question arose: What does a portfolio do when it encompasses both writing and information literacy? Furthermore, what role does rhetoric play in this combination? Our solution was two-fold. The first change was to tightly organize the assignment sequence so that the portfolio revolved solely around a single research project: every assignment was designed to contribute to it. This ensures that students do quite a bit of structured invention and research work long before they are expected to submit a term paper, annotated bibliography, or even an outline or proposal. The second change was to build both writing and information literacy practice into nearly every assignment as part of a more general rhetorical analysis. This combination is most evident in a series of roughly three-page assignments that ask students to reflectively develop a research strategy for finding a source on a topic they are potentially interested in writing on. Once found, students analyze the text based on a particular rhetorical concept (e.g., ethos, pathos, logos) and then highlight how their analysis might inform future research and writing on the topic. Organizing our assignment sequence around a recursively and reflectively developed research program allowed us to integrate research into the course as a central pillar of the class rather than as a technical add-on, as it had been configured in previous iterations of the course.

What emerged from this process was a version of ENGL 102 that both looked familiar and completely different. By productively blurring the distinctions between information literacy, writing, and rhetoric, we were able to remake ENGL 102's center. No element of the course feels like it is any more dedicated to one of these three elements than any of the others; in fact, it is difficult to divorce an iterative approach to research from the process of discovery through writing or rhetorical invention and persuasion. Doing this, though, required that our director let go of her vision of ENGL 102 (a course that she had redesigned only a few years earlier) enough to allow the difference of Information Literacy to do its work.

While this is a small slice of what was a massive institutional initiative, the example shows how the general education requirement sparked a unique intersection that enabled a productive reimagining of ENGL 102. Of course, not all of the intersections prompted by the wider overhaul were capable of being affirmed to the same positive effect. This is why I supplement, not supplant, approaches advanced by Micciche, Gunner, and Heard. Some dynamics would have been best responded to with a certain sensibility, others with tactical agility, and others were just plain frustrating and demanded critical attention (and, of course, these responses are almost always blurred with each other in some unique combination).

I further want to emphasize that it is very difficult, if not impossible, to verify whether or not our director was "really" affirming the situation in any final or empirical sense. After all, ENGL 102 is still taught as a rhetoric course, and one could make the argument that its information literacy component has, to a degree, been colonized by that more general rhetorical orientation. Yet, our director consistently configured the overhaul–and all of the various components it gathered–as an inventive opportunity. Our director's orientation to the otherness of INF folded back onto her to help cultivate an affective disposition that extended beyond her individual identity. My goal here is to highlight how an affirmative approach emphasizes the inventive potential the encounter made possible, for the information literacy requirement, the rhetorical instruction of writing in ENGL 102, and for the institutional inscription of our WPA.

Conclusions: We Don't Know What Administration Can Do

WPA scholarship has repeatedly drawn attention to the physical bodies of writing program directors. As Gunner put it in her WPA plenary address, they get "worn down, burned out, disappointed, and lonely" (Gunner "Heroic Bodies"). Most frustration narratives validate this generalization, focusing on individual persons and bodies and the impact they have on crafting our professional identities. That is, WPA scholarship of this vein mostly focuses on the effects that WPA work has on WPAs, thereby focusing on the interiority of individual people. This is important work. But, as I note above, Heard draws our attention away from just the state of the WPA-as-a-person and shows how an institutional position is distributed through and folds back onto its bureaucratic environment.

In many ways, Heard calls for a kind of a disruption of the WPA body as something siloed within universities to reveal where and how that body extends beyond itself, through and into the various pathways of university writing. An affirmative approach to administration affirms nothing more than this extended (or pre-individual, as I've been calling it) body of the WPA itself. Doing so puts our identity as WPAs at risk as it is distributed through and transformed by the heterogeneity of the WPA position. This risk, though, is not that of erasure; it is a continual process of becoming. Affirming one's identity as WPA is simultaneously a will-to-become-oneself-to-the-point-of-non-recognition. To echo and adapt Baruch Spinoza, we do not know what writing program administration can do, and this "not knowing" is in no way a lack, but the very possibility of becoming-WPA.

Works Cited

Althusser, Louis. *Lenin and Philosophy and Other Essays*. Monthly Review Press, 2001.

Association of American Colleges and Universities. *College Learning for the New Global Century A Report from the National Leadership Council for Liberal Education & America's Promise*. Distributed by ERIC Clearinghouse, 2007.

Bishop, Wendy, and Gay Lynn Crossley. "How to Tell a Story of Stopping: The Complexities of Narrating a WPA's Experience." *WPA*, vol. 19, no. 3, 1996, pp 70-79.

Brewer, Meaghan, and Kristen di Gennaro. "Naming What We Feel: Hierarchical Microaggressions and the Relationship between Composition and English Studies." *Composition Studies*, vol. 46, no. 2, 2018, pp. 15-34.

Certeau, Michel de. *The Practice of Everyday Life*. Translated by Steven Rendall, 3rd ed, U of California P, 2011.

Coburn, Leon. "Notes of a freshman Freshman Comp director *or* Lasciate ogni Esperanza void ch' entrate" *WPA*, vol. 5, no. 3, 1982, pp. 9-14.

Craig, Collin Lamount, and Staci Maree Perryman-Clark. "Troubling the Boundaries (De)Constructing WPA Identities at the Intersections of Race and Gender. *WPA*, vol. 34, no. 2, 2011, pp. 37-58.

—. "Troubling the Boundaries Revisited: Moving Toward Change as Things Stay the Same." *WPA*, vol. 39, no. 2, 2016, pp. 20-26.

DeGenaro, William. "Kurt Cobain, Writing Program Administrator." *WPA*, vol. 42, no.1, 2018, pp. 17-35.

Deitering, Anne-Marie, and Sara Jameson. "Step by Step through the Scholarly Conversation: A Collaborative Library/Writing Faculty Project to Embed Information Literacy and Promote Critical Thinking in First Year Composition at Oregon State University." *College & Undergraduate Libraries*, vol. 15, no. 1–2, 2008, pp. 57–79.

Deleuze, Gilles, and Félix Guattari. *A Thousand Plateaus: Capitalism and Schizophrenia*. Translated by Brian Massumi. U Minnesota P, 1987.

—. *Spinoza: Practical Philosophy*. Translated by Robert Hurley. City Lights Books, 1988.

Edbauer, Jenny. "Unframing Models of Public Distribution: From Rhetorical Situation to Rhetorical Ecologies." *Rhetoric Society Quarterly*, vol. 35, no. 4, 2005, pp. 5–24.

Gates Jr., Henry Louise. *The Signifying Monkey*. 25th Anniversary Ed. Oxford UP, 2014.

George, Diana Ed. *Kitchen Cooks, Plate Twirlers, & Troubadours: Writing Program Administrators Tell Their Stories*. Boynton/Cook, 1999.

Gunner, Jeanne. "Ideology, Theory, and the Genre of Writing Programs." *The Writing Program Administrator as Theorist*. Eds. Shirley K. Rose & Irwin Weiser. Boynton-Cook/Heinermann, 2002.

— "Heroic Bodies." WPA Annual Conference. University of North Carolina, Charlotte 14 July 2000. Plenary Address.

Hairston, Maxine. "The Winds of Change: Thomas Kuhn and the Revolution in the Teaching of Writing." *College Composition and Communication*. vol. 33, no. 1, 1982, pp. 76-88.

Heard, Matthew. "Cultivating Sensibility in Writing Program Administration." *WPA*, vol. 35, no. 2, 2012, pp. 38-54.

Holbrook, Sue Ellen. "Women's Work: The Feminizing of Composition." *Rhetoric Review*, vol. 9, no. 2, 1991, pp. 201–29.

Jackson, Rebecca, Jackie Grutsch McKinney, and Nicole I, Caswell. "Writing Center Administration and/as Emotional Labor." *Composition Forum*, vol. 34, Summer 2016.

Kelsie, Amber. "Blackened Debate at the End of the World." *Philosophy & Rhetoric*, vol. 52, no. 1, 2019, pp. 63-70.

Malenczyk, Rita. "Kitchen Cooks, Plate Twirlers, and Posers; or, the I's Have It." *WPA*, vol. 35, no. 2, 2012, pp. 184-89.

McGee, Sharon James. "Overcoming Disappointment: Constructing Writing Program Identity Through Postmodern Mapping." *Discord & Direction: The Postmodern Writing Program Administrator*. Eds, Sharon James McGee and Carolyn Handa. Utah State UP, 2005.

Micciche, Laura R. *Doing Emotion: Rhetoric, Writing, Teaching*. Boynton/Cook Publishers, 2007.

— "More than a Feeling: Disappointment and WPA Work." *College English*, vol. 64, no. 4, 2002, pp. 432-58.

Miller-Cochran, Susan. "Innovation Through Intentional Administration: Or, How to Lead a Writing Program Without Losing Your Soul." *WPA*, vol. 42, no. 1, 2018, pp. 107-122.

Muckelbauer, John. *The Future of Invention: Rhetoric, Postmodernism, and the Problem of Change*. SUNY P, 2008.

Nealon, Jeffrey. *Alterity Politics: Ethics and Performative Subjectivity*. Duke UP, 1998.

Sano-Franchini, Jennifer. "'It's Like Writing Yourself into a Codependent Relationship with Someone Who Doesn't Even Want You!' Emotional Labor, Intimacy, and the Academic Job Market in Rhetoric and Composition." *College Composition and Communication*, vol. 68, no. 1, 2016, pp. 98-124.

Smoke, Trudy. "Collaborating with Power: Contradictions of Working as a WPA." *WPA*, vol. 21, no. 2/3, 1998, pp. 92-100.

Spinoza, Benedictus de. *The Collected Works of Spinoza*. Translated by E. M. Curley, Princeton UP, 1985.

Politeness Profiles in the First-Year Composition Classroom

Pennie L. Gray

During peer review, students often exhibit resistance when asked to respond critically to their peers' writing. Most students tend to offer gentle critiques, especially when they personally know the peers whose writing they are reading. This tendency to be overly kind can be frustrating for instructors, yet there may be logical reasons for students' hesitancy to engage in critical peer review. This study explores students' peer review letters through the lens of linguistic politeness theory and illuminates one possible explanation for the reluctant peer review.

Benefits of the Peer Review Process

The peer review process, a mainstay of many composition classrooms in the United States, requires students to read one another's writing and offer—or attempt to offer—substantive critical feedback. However, the peer review process is somewhat complex and nuanced. For instance, as Donna Johnson and A. W. Roen note, the peer review process necessitates students' negotiation of the liminal space between helping their classmates improve their writing and simultaneously meeting the expectations of the instructor who assigned the peer review (34). Other factors also influence the peer review process: the age and experience of the students; the format of the peer review, whether electronic, face-to-face, or written; the social relationship of the peer reviewers, and more.

Nonetheless, many instructors turn to peer review as one way to give students more feedback than they are capable of generating themselves and as an avenue for involving students in the response process. As Ruiling Lu and Linda Bol found, using peer review in the composition classroom has its benefits: It lessens the instructor's workload and leads to better writing outcomes (101). Korey Lawson Ching points out that an additional benefit of the peer review process is that it minimizes the "binary distinction between teacher authority and student autonomy . . . and reconfigures the participation of students and teachers" in the composition classroom (314). By asking students to participate in the feedback process, the classroom environment can become more community oriented, a kind of "apprenticeship in which students participate alongside teachers" (314). Furthermore, peer review allows students to "take an active role in evaluating the work of other students" rather than remaining passive recipients of teacher commentary (314). Even more, by encouraging students to review one another's work, the peer review process can serve instructional purposes. As students compare their own work to that of their peers, they become more aware of their own writing tendencies and habits. This process thus gives them a window into areas of improvement in their own writing (Stellmack et al., 236).

Recent research by Kristi Lundstrom and Wendy Baker highlights the benefits of peer review not for the student being reviewed, but rather for the student doing the peer review. While the peer review process is intended primarily to help the student whose composition is being reviewed, there are additional learning benefits for the student who is serving as the peer reviewer (Nicol et al., 104). For one, the peer reviewer learns to make evaluative and reflective comments on another's work (Cho and Cho, 630). This type of critical thinking about another's work could transfer into thinking critically about the reviewer's own writing as well. In this way, students may engage in critical thinking as they "learn by explaining what makes peer texts good or bad, by identifying problems that exist in those peer texts, and then in devising ways in which those problems can be solved" (630).

Increased audience awareness is another benefit of the peer review process. Often, students write to an undefined audience; it can be difficult to move novice writers into the realm of writing to real audiences, but the peer review process provides one avenue for this shift. When students realize that one of their peers will be reading and commenting on their work, they begin to write differently. Lu and Bol found that students did, indeed, write more carefully when they knew other students would be reading and commenting on their work (101). In fact, students are compelled to imagine how others will view their writing and move out of their own realm to consider others' responses during the peer review process. As Cho and Cho state, "by reviewing peer drafts, student reviewers can develop a more accurate understanding of their readers" (631). Novice students may not have the ability to view their writing from a disembodied viewpoint, but the peer review process moves students toward this important shift by providing a much-needed alternative perspective (631).

The benefits of peer review have been well documented. In addition to the research of Stellmack et al., Nicol et al., and Cho and Cho, Philip Vickerman found that some students were able to "gain confidence in student-led discussion and independent learning" from the peer review process (227). Vickerman also found that student engagement increased through the peer review process as long as students' learning preferences and styles were taken into account. Loretto et al. noted that peer review was beneficial for students, especially when anonymity of peer reviewers was maintained. Yet, Yucel et al. concluded that while the peer review process improved students' "self-assessment skills for judging the quality of their *own* writing in the future" (983, emphasis added), students often remained largely unaware of this benefit. In spite of some variance as to the benefits of the peer review process (depending on the expertise of the peer reviewer), Yucel et al. noted that "*giving* feedback to peers might benefit a student as much as *receiving* feedback" on their own writing (971). Melissa M. Patchun and Christian D. Schunn and Andrew Nobel likewise concluded that there are a range of benefits for the student conducting the peer review but that there are variances as to the scope of those benefits. Nonetheless, the benefits of the peer review process are proven.

One aspect of peer review that has received limited attention is the role that politeness plays in the process. In spite of this limited attention, the social dynamics of peer review should not be overlooked. When students engage in peer review, they are engaging not only with a piece of written text, but also with the author of that text, whether directly or indirectly. Thus a consideration of the social nuances of the peer review process is warranted. For the purposes of this research, the role of politeness during peer review is explored in order to illuminate this layer of the socially-grounded peer review process.

Politeness Theory and Peer Review

According to Penelope Brown and Stephen C. Levinson, in all interactions, interlocutors have two particular wants or needs: the want to be unimpeded, referred to as negative face, and the want to be approved of in certain respects, referred to as positive face (58). These positive and negative face needs are addressed during social interactions as interlocutors respond to what they believe to be the face needs of their fellow interlocutors. However, it is inevitable that during social interactions, some actions will threaten the positive and negative face needs of the interlocutors—actions referred to as Face Threatening Acts (FTAs) (60). These FTAs are often mitigated through the use of politeness strategies referred to as positive or negative politeness.

Positive politeness, as the name indicates, is oriented toward the positive face needs of the hearer and thus "anoints" the positive face of the hearer (70). For instance, the speaker might say, "You are such a good writer. Would you mind helping me with my paper?" In this example, the speaker anoints the positive face of the hearer by acknowledging a positive quality that the hearer may claim for themselves. Negative politeness, on the other hand, is oriented toward the negative face of the hearer and as such is "avoidance-based" (70). Negative politeness often requires the speaker to acknowledge the imposition of the FTA through the use of apologies, self-effacement, deference, hedges, or implications of non-coercion (70). For instance, the speaker might say, "I know it's a lot to ask and you're terribly busy, but would you mind helping me with my paper?" These types of face-to-face examples of positive and negative politeness also map onto written demonstrations of politeness during peer review. For instance, in a written peer review, the student providing feedback on a peer's text might say something along the lines of "You did a wonderful job in your introduction," thus anointing the positive face of the author. For negative politeness, the peer reviewer might hedge criticisms by writing statements like, "You might want to think about changing this word here, but it's your call." However, there is a significant difference between verbal and written feedback: Written feedback can be more intentional, because the author has time to consider their word choice before sharing the feedback with the author, whereas speakers rarely have much time to consider carefully what they say. Thus, due to the increased intentionality evident in the written peer review (and the extant textual record of the exchange), the use of politeness strategies can be more easily identified and analyzed. These moments of politeness strategy use, located and locatable in text, are called tokens.

Brown and Levinson offer a formula for computing the weightiness or seriousness of any given FTA, whether written or spoken, which in turn informs the choice and degree of politeness strategies required for that particular situation (76). The formula is:

$W_x = D(S,H) + P(H,S) + R_x$

In this equation, W_x represents the relative weight or seriousness of the imposition and is calculated by considering three factors: the social distance between the speaker and hearer, represented by $D(S,H)$; the measure of the power the hearer has over the speaker, represented by $P(H,S)$; and the degree to which the FTA is weighted as an imposition within a given culture, represented by R_x (76).

Thus, the weightiness of politeness strategies any interlocutor chooses arises from a confluence of factors. A savvy interlocutor weighs each of the factors present in a social situation and, almost subconsciously and instantaneously, choose the politeness strategies that are appropriate given the unique social circumstance situated in the specific culture and context. In the composition classroom, the task of writing compositions and engaging in the peer review process remains constant for all students; the expectations of the writing assignments are most likely regulated by the course instructor by way of assignment descriptions. Likewise, the power differential—between students qua students—remains mostly constant, as does the power differential between teacher and student. However, what does not remain constant in the composition classroom is the social distance. The social distance students feel typically changes over the course of the semester as students come to know one another better. An examination of the social dynamics of peer review can reveal as-yet-unexplored layers to the peer review process, and politeness theory provides a meaningful framework for this examination. More specifically, the social distance aspect of politeness warrants careful consideration, especially in light of the ways students use positive and negative politeness tokens in the peer review process and what those politeness tokens might reveal about their comfort with the critique inherent in the peer review process.

Wolfson's Bulge Theory

Nessa Wolfson examined the interplay between politeness and social distance, and like Brown and Levinson, Wolfson provides a useful framework for analysis of peer review. Wolfson contended that we can examine speech acts to get at "the social strategies people in a given speech community use to accomplish their purposes—to gain cooperation, to form friendships, and to keep their world running smoothly" (31). Wolfson, using a middle-class American speech community, examined the differences in the kind and frequency with which interlocutors used politeness strategies. For her research, Wolfson focused on the social distance aspect of the weightiness formula offered by Brown and Levinson. In particular, she found that "the two extremes of social distance—minimum and maximum—seem to call forth very similar behavior, while relationships which are more toward the center showed marked differences" (32). Wolfson went on to say that, "the more status and social distance are seen as fixed, the easier it is for speakers to know what to expect of one another" (33). Furthermore, "what inequality of status and intimacy have in common is that in both situations, interlocutors know exactly where they stand with one another" (34). Based on these findings, Wolfson posited that people who are either intimates or strangers use fewer politeness strategies because their relationships are seen as fixed. On the other hand, people who are non-intimates and non-strangers tend to use more politeness strategies as they seek to solidify their relationship. Thus, Wolfson's Bulge Theory might be illustrated as in Figure 1. Of special note is Wolfson's finding—hearkening back to the research of Lynne D'Amico-Reisner—that "interlocutors who are in the Bulge almost never voice their disapproval of one another overtly" (35).

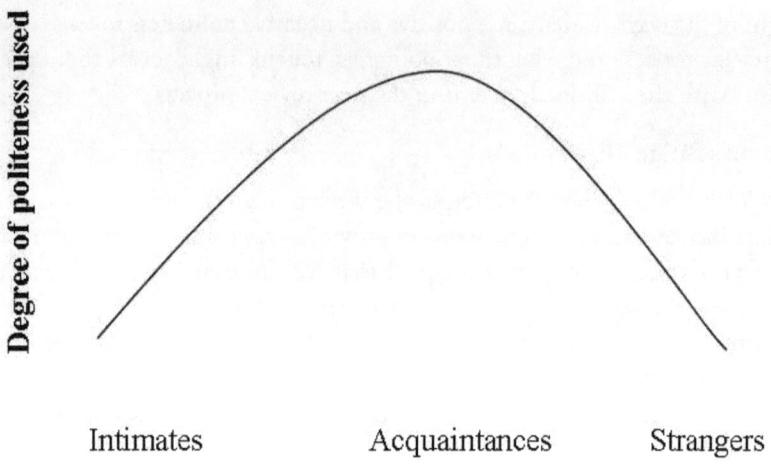

Figure 1.

Research on the interplay between peer review and politeness theory has appeared in a number contexts. Syavash Nabarany and Kellogg S. Booth examined the use of politeness strategies through an analysis of non-anonymous peer reviews of academic papers by science and technology scholars. They considered factors such as anonymity, experience, and expertise in the peer review process and found that criticisms were mitigated by at least one politeness strategy 85 percent of the time (1053) and that an area not typically mitigated by politeness was grammatical errors (1054). Donna Johnson and Duane H. Roen likewise explored politeness strategies during peer review and found that graduate students' use of politeness strategies (in the form of compliments) varied according to gender, with women offering more compliments than men (38). Lu and Bol, in their study of online anonymous versus identifiable peer review with college students, found that anonymity resulted in more candid and valuable feedback for the students (110). Each of these studies illuminated an important consideration for peer review using the lens of politeness theory.

What none of these studies considered, however, was how first-year college students engage in peer review. First-year college students have far less academic writing experience than graduate students and established scholars; they are likewise less acclimated to higher education and the crucial role peer review plays in forwarding academic knowledge. Thus, this study explores the non-anonymous peer review process of first-year college students using Brown and Levinson's framework of linguistic politeness theory and Wolfson's bulge theory. This study analyzed the peer review letters of thirteen students in a first-year composition course, which revealed as-yet-unexamined aspects of the peer review process that may be applicable to other first-year composition classrooms.

Context and Methods

This IRB-approved study was conducted in a first-year composition course offered at a small, private, liberal arts university in the midwestern United States. First-year composition courses at this university are topic-centered, which means that each course focuses on a particular subject with students writing all their compositions about that subject. The courses are designed as discussion-focused classes that engage students in intellectual inquiry and develop students' ability to grapple with and evaluate competing ideas about the topic of the course. Additionally, the courses are writing intensive, so parallel goals include engaging students in all stages of the writing process, helping students identify various audiences and purposes for writing, giving students the opportunity to use writing as a means of discovery and invention, and giving students significant practice in writing both formally and informally. The topic of the course in this study was homelessness, so one aspect of the course was devoted to the study of homelessness while other aspects were focused on developing students' writing and critical thinking skills.

There were a number of unique characteristics of this particular group of students that warrant mention. First, of the thirteen students (six men and seven women), five men were part of the same athletic team and as such had arrived on campus one week before classes began to take part in pre-season practice. These student-athletes had the opportunity to form a type of in-group within the larger classroom group and had already begun to share some familiarity characteristics such as inside jokes and friendly teasing. Additionally, the entire class spent the first three days on campus traveling as a cohort from one orientation activity to the next, so by the time I met them for the first time, they were at least familiar with one another (if not somewhat cohesive as a group). Furthermore, these students were my first-year advisees, so I spent considerable time with them—one-on-one and as a group—as they navigated the course selection process and acclimated themselves to campus living. Finally, students who typically enroll at this small private university come from middle to upper-middle class families and have a history of academic success. All these factors contributed to the unique environment of this particular composition classroom and what transpired over the course of the semester.

The methods used in this study were drawn from qualitative research methods, including the self-study framework and content analysis. Self-study is characterized by a "spiral of questioning, framing, revisiting of data, and reframing of a researcher's interpretations" (Samaras 11). Thus, self-study requires an open stance in which the teacher-researcher considers outside views, fresh possibilities, and a unique application of existing theoretical constructs. In self-study, the teacher-researcher discovers new knowledge through disciplined, systematic inquiry coupled with intentional reflection (14).

More specifically, self-study is focused on the unveiling of pedagogical nuances. It holds an "orientation toward one's practice. It is a questioning attitude toward the world, leading to inquiry conducted within a disciplined framework" (Freeman 8). Self-study is somewhat organic to the classroom in that, according to Samaras, "Research is what teachers do" (9). Teachers conduct research informally every day in the classroom as they try new strategies and attempt to understand better some aspect of their own unique practice in the classroom (9). Therefore, using the self-study framework, I examined my pedagogical decision to employ peer review in my first-year composition course and reconsidered my expectations of how this process should unfold.

Bolstering this self-study framework, I drew on content analysis as a complementary qualitative research method that allowed me to conduct an analysis of two sets of peer review letters students wrote for the course. As Steve Stemler describes, content analysis is a systematic technique for organizing many words in a text into specific categories for analysis (1). A robust content analysis goes far beyond a mere noting of the frequency of word choice and instead examines the context in which particular words or phrases are used. The process then enables the researcher to assign each word or phrase to specific and nuanced categories; from these categories, researchers can describe and discover trends in a given text from which inferences and conclusions can be made.

Students in this course were required to write four compositions, at least three of which were research papers, meaning the texts had to cite at least one academic source to support a claim. For all four compositions, students received audio recorded feedback on their drafts from me. On the second and third compositions, students participated in a peer review conference and received written peer review letters from two of their classmates. The peer review groups were randomly selected but in such a way as to assure that the peer review groups were different both times. To analyze the data for this study, I read through the first set of peer review letters to note whether any particular trends stood out to me. Then, using a content analysis framework, I developed a list of specific patterns that were emerging from the data. With politeness theory in mind, I began to look for evidence of any politeness strategies used by the students, noting examples of the use of positive politeness and negative politeness, broadly defined. When I found evidence of a student using a particular politeness strategy, I color-coded the strategy using a different color for each broad category (e.g., positive politeness, negative politeness). I then conducted the same content analysis for the second set of peer review letters. In all, the first set of data included 26 peer review letters, each approximately one double-spaced page long. The entire data set equaled 6854 words. The second set of peer review letters likewise included 26 letters and 6673 words in all and was analyzed using the same codes. Once the politeness strategies were highlighted, I then conducted additional analyses to identify more specific trends that were emerging. Finally, I compiled all similar strategies into separate documents for further analysis, which revealed illuminating trends.

Three dimensions of the students' compositions are important for the context of politeness strategy analysis: the texts were multimodal; the texts addressed diverse aspects of the course topic; and many of the texts were quite personal. The genres and modes of each composition the students wrote over the course of the semester varied widely. Because writing in the real world is not always constrained and proscribed, a number of years ago I shifted from having all students write using the same genre and type of papers. Therefore, for the focus class in this study, I asked the students to define their own writing tasks by submitting a proposal for each composition in which they defined an audience for their composition and a purpose for their writing. After receiving instructor feedback and guidance on their proposals, students set about composing.

As might be expected, the resultant compositions were quite diverse. Among the topics students chose were the following: homelessness as a choice; preconceived ideas about homelessness; mental illness and its connection to homelessness; assistance available to the homeless; the omission of homeless women, specifically homeless mothers, from most texts about homelessness; the potentially negative effects of homeless shelters. But beyond the varied topics of the compositions, students also pursued a host of modes for their topics as they sought to align their topic with the most suitable genre. Some students wrote short stories and vignettes, while others chose multimedia genres such as websites and YouTube music videos. Perhaps the riskiest composition was a three-song series a student wrote, performed, recorded, and shared with the class, a project that reflected an encounter the student had with a homeless street musician when he was five years old.

Due to the personal nature of some of the compositions and especially because the students designed the writing tasks themselves, students aptly surmised that, during peer review, they were responding not only to a composition, but also—and perhaps more importantly—to their peers. In order to build and preserve cohesiveness and rapport, students responded to their peers' compositions tactfully and kindly as was evidenced in their peer review letters. Yet, at the same time, students were aware of the fact that the peer review process was subject to the scrutiny of the instructor. For this course, I gave students course credit for the peer review letters they wrote to one another. These grades were holistic and served as an affirmation that each student participated fully in the peer review process.

Prior to writing their peer review letters, though, students offered face-to-face feedback to each other during peer review sessions in class. They met in small groups, asked one person to read the draft aloud, and then gave some preliminary feedback and suggestions. Only after the face-to-face sessions did peer reviewers take home a draft of the compositions and formalize their feedback in page-long peer review letters articulating suggestions for improvement. These suggestions, which were required in the written assignment description, presented opportunities for FTAs (e.g. offending their peers or implying that they lacked writing ability). This type of peer review assignment placed students in an uneasy conundrum: As Johnson and Yang note, "to be overly critical (during peer review) might offend a classmate, but not to be sufficiently critical would not meet the requirements of the assignment" (102). Thus, students often use caution when navigating social distance within this challenging rhetorical task. Rather than offend their peers, Jesnek noted that most students prioritize social acceptance and the protection of peer relationships over offering critical feedback during peer review (23), and Brammer and Rees found similar results in their research on the peer review process in that building rapport among classmates is crucial to productive peer review. Students rely on "a sense of shared community in order to develop dialogues of trust and to build confidence in their classroom peers" (81).

Results of Peer Review Letter Analysis

In the context of this course, my design of this embedded peer review task, and the multiple dynamics of student compositions, self-study and content analysis of the peer review letters yielded two trends in terms of politeness strategies used by students: (1) the use of exaggerated praise and (2) the use of hedging, specifically the minimization of imposition and expertise.

Exaggerated Praise

My own observations of students during peer review followed by an analysis of their peer review letters confirmed that students pushed back against my requirement that they respond critically to one another's compositions. Through my content analysis coding, I noted the frequency with which students used positive and negative politeness strategies and found that students were highly encouraging of one another not only face-to-face, but especially in their written peer review letters. They mentioned their appreciation for the writing of their peers, and they also exaggerated their praise by being far more complimentary of one another than was warranted based on the quality of the compositions.

For instance, in response to a composition about mental illness and homelessness, a student wrote, "The way you describe homelessness is the perfect way to begin in my opinion." In responding to a composition using the found poem genre, a student wrote, "I really enjoyed your poem" and later, "I LOVE that final line you put in there about how at the end of the day, you're still a man. . . It's brilliant." To the student who wrote a three-song series, the peer reviewer commented, "I really love the idea of this piece. It's so original and something I myself never would have thought about doing. I really enjoyed the first song." This same student later wrote, "You can't even tell that you never really have written lyrics before. They flow well throughout your songs and none of them need changing." Another student who wrote a children's book about Hurricane Katrina's effect on New Orleans received this feedback: "First off, really great job! I really love your idea for the children's book." Responding to a student's poem, one peer reviewer wrote, "I loved the ending. It was really good. And I especially loved how you ended with the word period. I thought that was clever."

From these samples of exaggerated praise, I teased out specific words students used; among other things, I looked for words that fell into the category of superlatives. I looked for statements that indicated strongly-worded positive praise. The frequent use of the word "really" to intensify praise was also quite common in the peer review letters as was some effusive praise to indicate their "love" of their peers' compositions and their belief that aspects of the work were "perfect," and in one case, "brilliant." While the argument could be made that the frequent use of the word really was simply a characteristic of the writing style of that particular group of students, what is striking is that most peer review letters contained the word "really" to emphasize a positive comment, and all letters included intensified praise and lofty compliments. It seemed that students chose not to abide by the guidance of the assignment description, which urged them to ask questions, comment on the organization, and go beyond mere praise. While some students did delve into some more substantial critiques, few offered any negative comments at all. This suggests that students prioritized their peers' feelings about the peer review letters more than my preference that they offer more substantial and instructive feedback. The students' responses point to not only their use of politeness strategies, but also the ways in which they were attuned to social dynamics of the class.

Minimization of Imposition and Expertise

Another trend that emerged in the peer review letters was the recurring use of the word "just" and other wording that minimized the suggestions for further work they recommended. I first noticed the pattern emerging from the peer review letters upon my initial reading of the letters. In response to the finding that students were hesitant to provide suggestions, I returned to the letters to look for examples of how students appeared to minimize their own feedback and authority; I found that nearly all students used the word "just" to accomplish this mitigation of imposition and authority. For instance, in response to a student-developed website focused on famous people who were once homeless, the peer reviewer wrote, "I would suggest just doing a real basic search on homeless people and seeing what facts come up and going off of those." In this case, the reviewer was minimizing the imposition of the suggestion through the use of the word "just." In a paper about legislation to protect homeless college students, the peer reviewer wrote, "There were just a couple of words and commas that I added." In this instance, the effort needed to correct the author's errors was minimized through the use of the word "just," which indicated that the revisions were small. Likewise, the revision imposition was minimized for a paper about Skid Row when the reviewer wrote, "I would just reread through your paper and make sure you're not being too repetitive with that." The reviewer later continued saying, "You're not obligated to use my corrections, they're just suggestions." Among the other comments added by peer reviewers were: "Also just a little thing: make sure you're putting your periods after your parenthetical references rather than at the end of the sentence" and "After reading your composition piece, I have just a couple of slight suggestions."

In their peer review letters, students were using words like "just" to minimize the work they were suggesting their peers do during revision. Perhaps students were reluctant to ask their classmates to significantly alter their work and thus wanted to make it sound as if very little needed to be done to make the compositions stronger. In contrast to Nabarany and Booth's finding that non-anonymous peer reviews did not hedge feedback on grammar errors, the students in this composition classroom did just that.

However, my analysis revealed that students used the word "just" and other hedges in a slightly different way in other parts of their peer review letters. In some instances, students used the word "just" to minimize their own authority or expertise. For example, in responding to a composition about children and homelessness, a peer reviewer used the word "just" along with the phrase "I'm not judging you or anything" to offer feedback. She wrote, "Also, just a side note, this last page is when it really starts to be evident that you're sleepy and still writing, so check that out. I'm not judging or anything, just letting you know." Another peer reviewer commented, "This is just my opinion. Feel free to leave the sentences the way they are if you like." Another example of the minimization of a student's expertise was offered on a paper about the causes of homelessness: "Let me first say that any changes that I made in the paper were just ways that I thought would possibly make it flow a little more. You're not obligated to use my corrections. They're just suggestions." And finally, one peer reviewer repeatedly minimized their authority and expertise by saying, "Feel free to completely ignore these changes. They are just suggestions." These examples indicate that students were reluctant to exercise authority over their peers by implying that they had greater expertise—whether on subject matter, style, grammar, or other writing concerns— than their peers.

These examples show that students took great pains to use politeness strategies during the peer review process. In the first set of examples, students offered exaggerated praise to their peers and their peers' compositions, and in so doing, anointed their peers' positive face. While Brown and Levinson specifically caution against quantifying politeness strategies, it was nonetheless difficult to ignore the fact that students used many positive politeness intensifiers in their peer review letters. In all, for the first set of peer review letters on the first composition, students used 70 positive politeness phrases or sentences in 26 peer review letters. Additionally, students used the word "really" as a positive intensifier 18 times. Put simply, students used the word "really" to add emphasis to a positive statement addressed to their peer's positive face. Certainly, in some contexts the use of the word "really" was used as a colloquialism, but the ubiquitous use of the word to intensify positive politeness during peer review was difficult to dismiss outright.

In the second set of peer review letters, students used 139 positive politeness phrases and sentences in 26 letters. Additionally, they used the word "really" as a positive politeness intensifier 45 times. From the first peer review letter to the second, students nearly doubled their use of positive politeness phrases and sentences and more than doubled their use of the word "really" to emphasize their praise.

But students went beyond the use of positive politeness strategies; they also used negative politeness strategies. As previously noted, students made considerable use of the word "just," which can be categorized as a hedge. As Brown and Levinson state, "Normally, hedges are a feature of negative politeness . . . but some hedges can have this positive-politeness function as well, most notably (in English): sort of, kind of, like, in a way" (116). More specifically, hedges can be used to soften an FTA that involves a suggestion or criticism. These hedges are categorized as redressive actions: actions that give face to the addressee and that counteract potential face damage by highlighting the shared goals of the interlocutors (69-70). Additionally, these hedges acknowledge the negative face needs of the interlocutor and indicate a reluctance to impede the other's freedom of action.

The first way students used words like "just" was to minimize the FTA to the negative face of the peer. This was especially evident when students made suggestions for changes in their peers' compositions. Students sought to soften the blow of the imposition and to minimize the revision work they were suggesting. These kinds of comments are considered off-record comments and seek to minimize the imposition of the suggestion (Brown and Levinson 176, 214). A colloquial way of conceptualizing these types of comments is to think of them as the students' way of saying, "It's no big deal, but . . . ." The suggestion that accompanies the use of this type of hedge is thus framed as only a minor revision requiring little of the writer.

Students also used the word "just" to signify their own reluctance to assert their authority over their peers' writing, perhaps to minimize their social distance from one another. This type of mitigation served to help students create a certain camaraderie, a cohesiveness amongst themselves that downplayed the differences in expertise between them. It may have allowed students to remain at the same social level and could be thought of as a self-deprecating move that served to align the reviewer and the reviewed. A colloquial way to conceptualize these types of comments is to think of them as a way for the student to say, "But hey, what do I know?" These mitigations fall under what Brown and Levinson might refer to as an "out" by making it clear that the peer reviewer does not expect the writer to follow the suggestion unless the writer wants to do so (72). Based on these trends, it appeared that students took my mandate of the critical peer review letter and shaped it into something that better met their needs in the social context of the classroom. As students sought to solidify their relationships as classmates, they took great pains to avoid offending their peers through the peer review process. According to Wolfson's Bulge Theory, students were not intimates nor were they strangers, and they acknowledged and navigated this liminal space by using a great many politeness strategies.

A serendipitous yet important finding from this study involved the ways students learned about genre from one another. One student created an informative video, and two additional students also did so after peer reviewing the original student's work. After seeing a newsletter one student created for a project about resources for homeless citizens, another student (who was a nursing major) created a magazine with a series of articles about health services for the homeless. Another student was impressed with his peer's website development and tried his hand at that genre for his next composition. In creating, sharing, and reviewing a wide range of genres and modes, students were exposed to new ideas about textual creation that they later tried out themselves. This phenomenon reflects an important and additional benefit of the peer review process.

Conclusions and Pedagogical Implications

Based on these findings, I surmise that students used peer review to create a more secure, stable social environment in the composition classroom through the use of politeness strategies. Given that all peer review letters contained some examples of positive politeness and hedging, there is evidence of a consistent use of politeness strategies by all the students. In other words, students created a constellation of politeness strategies unique to the context and task at hand—a politeness profile of sorts. Drawing from a wide range of possibilities, most students landed on the same few strategies to respond to their peers' writing: they exaggerated their praise, they minimized the amount of work they were suggesting, and they downplayed their own authority or expertise. This particular politeness profile arose from the needs and goals of the students as they navigated FTAs in that particular writing context. Not only did students draw from many available politeness strategies, they used those strategies in varying degrees in order to support the risks they saw their classmates taking. Students attempted to support their peers' efforts as they engaged in risky writing tasks, tasks that their peers had designed and attempted to fulfill themselves. Thus, students recast the peer review as a social endeavor through their use of politeness strategies—a purpose all their own and, in some instances, contrary to the requirements of the assignment prompt.

If my students generated their own politeness profiles, it stands to reason that other students or groups of students will develop unique politeness profiles as well, a constellation of strategies that may differ from those evident in my classroom. An analysis of the types and frequency with which students use politeness strategies, contextualized by attention to specific dimensions of the writing examined like multimodality, topicality, and personal/affective investments, may help instructors align their expectations of the peer review process with what students will most likely do quite naturally. By attending to how students use politeness strategies in socially threatening environments such as the peer review, instructors are better positioned to support classroom cohesiveness and implement activities that strengthen the sense of safety and trust in the classroom.

As part of this self-study, I have reflected on my pedagogy and changed the way I design and conduct peer review to incorporate the study's insights into how students negotiate social distance, navigate politeness through FTAs, and encounter different modes and genres. Rather than require students to critique their peers' writing, I now ask the author of the composition to articulate the kind of feedback they want. The peer reviewer then shapes their feedback according to that request. And, more importantly, I tell students that the peer review process is designed to help not only the author, but also the peer reviewer. Prompted by students' adoption of the modes and genres of their peers, I now ask students to look at their peers' writing and notice what the author is doing so that they can use some of the same ideas in their own work. More importantly, by allowing students the freedom to bolster one another, I can reframe the peer review process as an activity that is and should be at least as beneficial for those acting as the peer reviewer as for the one receiving the peer review.

Works Cited

Brammer, Charlotte, and Mary Rees. "Peer Review from the Students' Perspective: Invaluable or Invalid?" *Composition Studies*, vol. 35, no. 2, 2007, pp. 71-85.

Brown, Penelope, and Stephen C. Levinson. *Politeness: Some Universals in Language Usage*. Cambridge University Press, 1987.

Ching, Kory Lawson. "Peer Response in the Composition Classroom: An Alternative Genealogy." *Rhetoric Review*, vol. 26, no. 3, 2007, pp. 303-19.

Cho, Young and Kwangsu Cho. "Peer Reviewers Learn from Giving Comments." *Interaction Science*, vol. 39, 2011, pp. 629-43.

Freeman, Don. *Doing Teacher Research: From Inquiry to Understanding*. Heinle and Heinle Publishers, 1998.

Jesnek, Lindsey M. "Peer Editing in the 21st Century College Classroom: Do Beginning Composition Students Truly Reap the Benefits?" *Journal of College Teaching & Learning*, vol. 8, no. 5, 2011, pp. 17-24.

Johnson, Donna M., and A. W. Yang. "Politeness Strategies in Peer Review Texts." *Pragmatics and Language Learning*. Eds. Lawrence F. Bouton and Yamuna Kachru. Division of English as an International Language Intensive English Institute, 1990.

Johnson, Donna M., and Duane H. Roen. "Complimenting and Involvement in Peer Reviews: Gender Variation." *Language in Society*, vol. 21, 1992, pp. 27-57.

Loretto, Adam, et al. "Secodary Students' Perceptions of Peer Review of Writing." *Research in the Teaching of English*, vol. 51, no. 2, 2016, pp. 134-161.

Lu, Ruiling, and Linda Bol. "A Comparison of Anonymous versus Identifiable e-Peer Review on College Student Writing Performance and the Extent of Critical Feedback." *Journal of Interactive Online Learning*, vol. 6, no. 2, 2007, pp. 100-15.

Lundstrom, Kristi, and Wendy Baker. "To Give is Better than to Receive: The Benefits of Peer Review to the Reviewer's Own Writing." *Journal of Second Language Writing*, vol. 18, 2009, pp. 30-43.

Mills, Sara. "Class, Gender, and Politeness." *Journal of Pragmatics*, vol. 24, 2004, pp. 381-92.

Nabarany, Syavash, and Kellogg S. Booth. "The Use of Politeness Strategies in Signed Open Peer Review." *Journal of the Association for Information Science and Technology*, vol. 66, no. 5, 2015, pp. 1048-64.

Nicol, David, et al. "Rethinking Feedback Practices in Higher Education: A Peer Review Perspective." *Assessment and Evaluation in Higher Education*, vol. 39, no. 1, 2014, pp. 102-22.

Noble, Andrew. "Formative Peer Review: Promoting Interactive, Reflective Learning, or the Blind Leading the Blind." *University of Detroit Mercy Law Review*, vol. 94, no. 3, 2017, pp. 441-58.

Patchun, Melissa M., and Christian D. Schunn, "Understanding the benefits of Providing Peer Feedback: How Students Response to Peers' Texts of Varying Quality." *Instructional Science*, vol. 43, 2015, pp. 591-614.

Samaras, Anastasia P. *Self-study Teacher Research: Improving Your Practice through Collaborative Inquiry.* Sage Publications, Inc, 2011.

Stellmack, Mark A., et al. "Review, Revise, and Resubmit: The Effects of Self-Critique, Peer Review, and Instructor Feedback on Student Writing." *Teaching of Psychology*, vol. 39, no. 4, 2012, pp. 235-44.

Wolfson, Nessa. "The Bulge: A Theory of Speech Behavior and Social Distance." *Second Language Discourse: A Textbook of Current Research*. Ed. Jonathon Fine. Ablex Publishing Co., 1988, pp. 21-38.

Yucel, Robyn, et al. "The Road to Self-Assessment: Exemplar Marking before Peer Review Develops First-Year Students' Capacity to Judge the Quality of a Scientific Report." *Assessment and Evaluation in Higher Education*, vol. 39, no. 8, 2014, pp. 971-86.

Stemler, Steve. "An Overview of Content Analysis." *Practical Assessment, Research, and Evaluation*, vol. 7, no. 17, 2001, pp. 1-6.

Vickerman, Philip. "Student Perspectives on Formative Peer Assessment: An Attempt to Deepen Learning." *Assessment and Evaluation in Higher Education*, vol. 34, no. 2, 2009, pp. 221-30.

Course Designs

Eng 7980: Learning Transfer in History and Theories of Composition

Ryan P. Shepherd, David T. Johnson, Sue Fletcher, Courtney A. Mauck, and Christopher J. Barber

Course Description

ENG 7980: History and Theories of Composition (HTC) is a course required for all MA and PhD students in rhetoric and composition at Ohio University.[1] This section of HTC was designed with two specific goals in mind. The first was to introduce students to multiple theories of composition, and the second was to not only teach but also to facilitate learning transfer. Ultimately, students would each create their own "theory" of composition. Class content was designed to connect to contexts outside of the immediate classroom setting—specifically to students' other classes, research projects, and teaching. Class assignments were designed to draw outside content into the class as well as to push class content into teaching and research.

This course design has been co-written by the instructor of HTC (Ryan) and four graduate students who took the class in fall 2017 (David, Sue, Courtney, and Chris). What follows is an extension of class content. David, Sue, Courtney, and Chris helped Ryan to reflect on the curriculum and update it based on what they learned about learning transfer.

Institutional Context

The curriculum for both the MA and PhD is diverse, including content on teaching, research methods, and theory. Both programs include courses outside of rhetoric and composition, such as an introduction to English studies, a literature course, and a course in critical theory. The programs have also been moving toward a specialization in cultural rhetorics.

The decision to study and to facilitate transfer in HTC came from Ryan's observation that students often perceive content in different courses as unconnected. In particular, as a scholar in rhetoric and composition, Ryan often saw connections between his research, theoretical readings, and classroom practice, but he also observed that graduate students struggled to make those same connections. Ryan hoped that HTC might help graduate students do three

---

1. You can find the syllabi and course calendars for each Course Design essay on the *Composition Studies* website at https://compstudiesjournal.com/.

things: recognize that a tension was taking place between their classes taken and taught; recognize connections across scholarly contexts; and seek out—or even create—those connections. Ryan saw this facilitation as an opportunity to connect the "delivered, lived, and experienced curricula" of graduate education as explored by Kara Taczak and Kathleen Blake Yancey (140) and designed the course content to include transfer from the very first day and to build toward more robust and critical connections as the semester progressed. The course highlighted learning transfer early in the semester, but students did not do readings on transfer theory until roughly the final third of the class.

Theoretical Rationale

The rationale for the course design grew out of Ryan's research into learning transfer at the undergraduate level (Shepherd) and the connections that learning transfer theory has with scholarship on teaching at the graduate level. Many studies have explored learning transfer models in first-year composition, such as Linda S. Bergmann and Janet Zepernick's exploration of disciplinarity in FYC, Ronda Leathers Dively's standardization of FYC for TA training, Douglas Downs and Elizabeth Wardle's theoretical framework for Writing about Writing (WAW), and Liane Robertson, Kara Taczak, and Kathleen Blake Yancey's earlier work that serves as a precursor to the Teaching for Transfer model. Many of these texts, and others written about transfer, note the benefits of reflection and metacognition for learning transfer. For example, Gerald Nelms and Ronda Leathers Dively position reflection as a means of helping students overcome roadblocks to transferring knowledge between FYC and major courses, and Rebecca S. Nowacek includes reflection as a major component of helping to make students "agents of integration."

Reflection is also often presented as a major component of graduate education, but this reflection is never explicitly expressed as a means of facilitating learning transfer for graduate students. For example, Michael Stancliff and Maureen Daly Goggin present reflection as a critical component of TA training. And Chris M. Anson and Susan K. Miller-Cochran expressly try to build "connections among disciplines, students, and the community while incorporating new approaches that will help make graduate education more relevant to the world outside of academia" (p. 39). In both cases, transfer theory can be easily connected to the methods for graduate teaching, but learning transfer is not directly referenced in either case. In the design of HTC, Ryan attempted to incorporate learning transfer into the class design while simultaneously attempting to keep these elements of reflection and connection. His hope was to use learning transfer theory to help graduate students make classroom learning more readily available and applicable in students' out-of-class scholarly pursuits, such as teaching and self-directed research.

The course design was particularly influenced by the Teaching for Transfer (TFT) model of first-year composition developed by Kathleen Blake Yancey, Liane Robertson, and Kara Taczak in *Writing Across Contexts*. In this model, students are introduced to several rhetorical concepts critical to composition studies and asked to develop their own theories of writing. HTC also followed a similar pattern. Course content was focused around several important concepts in the field, such as social construction, feminism, "error," multimodality, threshold concepts, and, of course, learning transfer. Students were then asked to use learning from the class (and outside of class) to build a theory of composition that included their positions on teaching, research, and theory as well as how those areas intertwined. This final project was very similar to the TFT model's theory of writing presented by Yancey, Robertson, and Taczak (56-58).

Also like TFT, course content was built around the "theory" assignment. Early in the course, Ryan asked students 11 questions related to composition and composition theory (see Appendix 1). These questions specifically encouraged students to take an inventory of their current knowledge and to recognize areas that they may not have considered in their own teaching and research. The questions focused on teaching, research, and threshold concepts prompted them to think beyond the immediate context of the course. Ideally, students would use examples from other classes, their own teaching, and their "extracurriculum" (Gere) to answer the questions early on. The intent was to draw on their delivered, lived, and experienced curricula: that is to say, class content, learning beyond the class, and self-sponsored learning, respectively.

Students in the course returned to these 11 questions about teaching and research regularly throughout the course in discussion, in activities, and in specific projects. The questions were asked on the first day of class and at the midpoint of the semester. They were often brought up in class discussions to keep them on students' minds. Ryan attempted to use these questions as a stand-in for the "key terms" that scaffold the TFT model (Yancey, Robertson, and Taczak 33-35).

In addition to the final project, the course asked students to complete three smaller projects that connected their class studies to research beyond the class. These were also designed to facilitate transfer and to be "a wide-open space that graduate students feel welcome to explore" (Mack 435). The Expansion Project asked students to choose a single topic from the class and include additional articles on that topic. The goal of this project was to help with research skills but also to allow students to bring in areas of interest. The Context Project asked students to connect a single reading from the class to the context in which it was written. The goal was to get students to think about the influences (personal, institutional, social, and disciplinary) that influence how research and teaching are done. The Gap Project furthered these goals by asking students to fill in a "gap" not covered in the assigned class readings. The goal was to encourage students to connect their own research interests to class material. All of these projects were designed to help students to expand beyond obvious class content and to think of their research and teaching as larger and more expansive. The projects were designed to give students agency in what they chose to learn. As Anson and Miller-Cochran point out, "[t]he scholarship of teaching and learning in higher education overwhelmingly supports instructional models in which students play an active role in the construction of their own knowledge and expertise through problem-solving activities" (40), and these three projects sought to do that. Ryan also saw these three projects as helping to build students' theories of composition by engaging with their own specific research interests.

These early documents were intended to allow for what Yancey, Robertson, and Taczak call "critical incidents" (5). Critical incidents are situations where students find that their current theories about learning or content are not working. While these situations may initially feel negative to a student, they ultimately allow them to retheorize the content (or their learning) and to create new theories that are more effective. Ryan had hoped that the class would be a safe place for critical incidents to occur.

Readings for the class built toward the focus on transfer and provided inspiration for their theories of composition. The first half of the semester focused on history and broader theories of composition. The goals of these readings were to prepare students to understand the later readings and to formulate their own theories of composition. Subsequent readings focused on contemporary theories of composition which then gave way to readings that focused explicitly on learning transfer (such as "Transfer of Learning" and excerpts from *Writing Across Contexts*) and readings that provided models for theories of composition (such as the "WPA Outcomes Statement for First-Year Composition" and the "Framework for Success in Postsecondary Writing").

While no articles explicitly connect graduate education and transfer, this curriculum does build on articles that call for reflection as part of graduate education. Reflection is a key component of the "mindful abstracting" necessary for transfer (Salomon and Perkins 115). Dively calls for reflection as part of TA training, for example, stating that students should be able to "reflect critically on their pedagogical practices, to enact appropriate practices in future contexts, and to articulate the rationale behind these practices." The goal of the course in general, and the final project in particular, was to do these very things: help students connect practices and articulate why and how they are connected. Many others call for this type of reflection as part of graduate education—reflection is a critical part of suggestions from Dylan B. Dryer; Peter H. Khost, Debra Rudder Lohe, and Chuck Sweetman; Sally Barr Ebest;

and Anson and Miller-Cochran, to name a few. HTC was designed so that this reflective element was built into the class explicitly. Students were asked to make regular connections between areas of classroom content and to contexts outside of the classroom. They were asked to think about what they learned in the context of their own teaching and research in order to make the content more relevant to their learning outside of the class.

Critical Reflection

The five authors have approached this section not only as a personal reflection on the course but also as an opportunity to redesign the curriculum. Below, the four graduate student co-authors provide individual reflections on a key aspect of their experience of the course. By reflecting on class content, the student co-authors were able to continue to engage in learning transfer and consider how class content affected situations outside of the class. This reflection is followed by a section offering suggestions for improving the curriculum written by all five authors.

Critical Incidents - Courtney

As a first year PhD student in rhetoric and composition, this course was one of Courtney's first courses in the discipline. When Ryan had the class complete the eleven questions for the first time, she was confident. The first question was "How do you define composition?", which is a question for which she felt she had an answer. However, as the class continued through the questions, the sounds of her peers typing furiously around her became daunting. There were questions for which she didn't not have real answers, and that realization troubled her. Her initial perception of the questions was that they were a "test"—a test that she was certain she wouldn't pass. Even though the purpose of the questions was pretty explicit, Courtney couldn't shake the feeling of embarrassment as she turned in her seemingly subpar answers.

As someone who was new to the discipline, Courtney felt there was really no way to know much about transfer or to completely understand what was happening on that first day of class. However, around the midpoint in the semester, the class revisited the questions again. While this was still daunting, she realized suddenly that she had a new language with which to answer the questions. This was the first moment where something "clicked" in her brain, and she was able to see how the readings and assignments were impacting her views of teaching and research. Though the questions were at first a very negative thing for Courtney, she believes that the initial negative experience made the final outcome more rewarding. Transfer typically involves a "critical incident"—a moment of failure where your previous knowledge just doesn't work (Yancey, Robertson, and Taczak). At the time, Courtney didn't realize she was experiencing such a moment because she was overwhelmed by the feeling of needing to perform a certain way—to "pass the test"—a feeling that stemmed from her prior experience in graduate classes. By the end of the semester she was able to see that it was never a test at all, but it would have been helpful if this had been made clearer earlier in the semester. Though failure can be an important part of learning transfer, Courtney believes she would have benefited from a better understanding of the questions at the start of the semester, which might have prompted her to mindfully reflect and make connections across contexts earlier on.

Future Teaching Transfer - David

David began HTC as a third-year doctoral student and assistant WPA who was familiar with the course design, having had parallel experiences with a similar framework in a prior graduate class. For him, the most effective part of the course was the pedagogical transfer he was able to identify and apply from his familiarity with the idea of the course and the threshold concepts as organizing principles.

Prior to the HTC course, David had been in a graduate course with a similar structure where students were asked to define good writing. He felt inspired to design and implement a similar FYC course with an approach grounded in a discourse/social-epistemic paradigm. The broader FYC course goals included:

- Having students write across contexts
- Helping students understand writing as a socially mediated, value-laden practice
- Helping students consider their own discursive relationships and literate practices across material and digital environments
- Helping students learn something about rhetoric and composition as a field of study.

From David's perspective, the FYC course had not been structured effectively and was not as successful as he had hoped, because he did not connect students' existing knowledge and writing practices to concepts like the social and rhetorical nature of writing.

After taking the HTC course, he revised the original FYC course with threshold concepts at its core. *Naming What We Know* gave David an accessible set of conceptual and organizing principles that he was able to use so that his students would be able to better identify and concretize the rhetorical awareness, genre familiarity, and writing practices in which they were already engaging and use this awareness to form connections to the new rhetorical situations in which they were being asked to perform. The threshold concepts would become "baseplates" for revising assignments and his course structure, allowing David to refine the nebulous, decontextualized grounding from the original course for projects like literacy narratives and locally-grounded research proposals. In the terms outlined by Yancey, Robertson, and Taczak, the organization of David's course moved from an assemblage model to an integrated, remix model (5).

What David felt could be improved about the HTC course was a more directive push toward leaving his scholarly comfort zone. He understood and appreciated the scaffolding of the major projects to allow students to locate and fully contextualize a particular conversation of interest in the discipline; he did feel, however, that reframing the major assignments to allow for required, individual exploration of the development of the field could have been just as helpful toward a broader foundational knowledge base, particularly in a discipline where members are often expected to be "jacks of all trades."

Professionalization - Chris

Entering HTC as a first-year MA student, Chris did not have any substantive familiarity with rhetoric and composition as a discipline. This resulted in him experiencing a form of imposter syndrome and an embarrassment comparable to Courtney's when she faced the key questions on the first day of the seminar. It wasn't until these questions were revisited at the midway point of the semester that Chris realized the questions were not meant to serve as indicators of his competency as a scholar, but rather, were entry points into pivotal conversations through which the discipline has been gradually shaped and defined throughout its history. This revelation was engendered by readings and discussion questions which highlighted the evolution of key terms in the discipline over time (process, social construction, multimodality, etc.) and the disciplinary debates which shaped their meaning. Chris found that this approach helped him to articulate his own ideas and conceptualize the discipline as more than static historical events but instead as so many ongoing scholarly conversations. This resulted in a clearer sense of what being a rhetoric and composition scholar actually entails.

Where Chris encountered roadblocks, he learned a lot by getting feedback on his ideas from the more experienced PhD students in the course. Their participation in class discussions—and the continuation of these conversations outside of the classroom—supplemented his understanding of the historical disciplinary debates presented by the readings while also providing him with a model for how ideas are shared and discussed among those in the field. By the end of the semester, he felt that a type of community of practice had emerged. Through speaking to more experienced students, Chris came to place greater value on the cultivation of classroom relationships as useful learning tools, a practice which he continued to employ in graduate classes beyond HTC. This transfer of knowledge was facilitated by small-group discussions, peer-review activities (both of which took place during the second half of the seminar), and the recurring course requirement that students reflect on three things: the effectiveness of past learning practices; how these may be successfully adapted for concurrent transfer; and how they might be adapted for future learning contexts. Chris's continued utilization of these social learning practices beyond HTC may well be the result of backward-reaching reflection practices demanded by the course's underlying transfer methodology.

That said, Chris believes that, especially as a newly-arrived student, he would have benefitted from having established these peer-to-peer relationships during the earlier, anxiety-ridden stages of the course. Perhaps integrating earlier and more frequent opportunities for mentorship into the course, and actively facilitating the development of such beneficial relationships from the beginning, would have helped mitigate Chris's initial imposter syndrome.

Reflection - Sue

A critical part of the course was the systematic reflection and feedback. The Reading Response postings before class provided a low-stakes, liminal space where Sue processed the weekly readings into reflective responses, measured her understanding against that of her peers, and eagerly looked for the instructor's dialogue regarding the connections she had made to the week's readings. The instructor's feedback encouraged her confidence in the ability to use the language of the discipline as a novice scholar just beginning the PhD program.

The Expansion, Context, and Gap projects were set up with sufficient flexibility and permission to just grapple with content. By the time she completed the Gap project, Sue could see her own distinct theoretical approach crystalizing. She discovered she had a lot more previous knowledge and practice than she had perceived on the first day with the 11 questions. Learning transfer is one example of a concept she felt she intuitively knew and had practiced in her composition classrooms for many years, but it was a concept for which she had little theoretical reference and grounding. She admitted that she was not always clear on the relationship between the first three projects. Reflecting back, she now sees this was by design—to provide space and time to work through that liminal space of her own theory formation. By the time the class reached the final theory project, she was more comfortable sorting through the messiness to figure out where her theoretical leanings fit together. At the same time, the expectation that the theory project was more of a starting point for future work (rather than an endpoint) proved a perfect challenge for Sue; as a novice, the project provided a valuable transition for her future growth as a composition scholar. Now, some two years into her program, Sue recognizes that she gained confidence as a scholar through this course, and through the final project in particular. Having the additional opportunity to work with Ryan on this research project provided the space to critically reflect back on the course as she experienced it. She can see evidence of backward reaching transfer as she encountered subsequent courses in her PhD program. Having the opportunity for input on potential changes to the course further solidifies the value of this course design as a model for graduate education.

Redesigned Curriculum for History and Theories of Composition

In what follows, the five authors of this text have attempted to revise the course to make it more effective—to better facilitate learning transfer and to enhance student engagement. The lessons here can be used directly within the curriculum for HTC, of course, but the authors also hope that these discussions may be applicable to other graduate courses in composition studies as well.

By asking the graduate students to help in the course revision process, Ryan was hoping to continue to facilitate learning transfer. The graduate students have been able to reflect on how to make connections across contexts through a mindful consideration of the ways that the course could be improved. In addition, this redesign is answering a call by Richard Marback: "Simply encouraging graduate students to apply what they know or training them to theorize through practice is not enough. We need to consider how, in doctoral education, we create the conditions for the exercise of judgment to guide knowledge making in composition studies" (824). Because there is little research on graduate education in composition studies, methods for helping students exercise judgment are rare. The hope here is that the four graduate student co-authors are helping to guide knowledge making through their participation.

In this section, David, Sue, Courtney, and Chris help Ryan to propose three major changes to the course described above: the reflective questions should be introduced later, and their purpose should be explicit; "critical incidents" should be introduced as positive outcomes earlier in the semester; and transfer should be woven into the class in additional ways.

One of the biggest opportunities for revision in the original design of HTC was that the purpose for the questions (Appendix 1) was not articulated clearly or fully when they were first posed. Because students felt that they couldn't answer the questions fully or, in some cases, couldn't answer some questions at all, they were anxious about the content of the class. Because disposition can so greatly affect learning and learning transfer (see, for example, Driscoll and Wells; Driscoll and Powell), this anxiety could be an impediment. Obviously, this was not the purpose of the questions. The purpose was to encourage students to think about strengths and weaknesses in their knowledge and to serve as a starting point for making connections to other learning, research, and teaching contexts.

To make this purpose clearer, and to use the questions more effectively, the authors propose a set of practices for introducing the questions. The first is to leave the questions for the *second* day of the class instead of introducing them on the first. Students felt a bit overwhelmed on the first day—even before the questions were asked. For many students, like Chris, this was their first day in their first graduate class, so when they were asked these questions and couldn't answer, they felt unprepared. To further mitigate this anxiety, teachers are encouraged to discuss the questions extensively when they are introduced. Instructors should make clear that the questions are not a test, that there is no possibility of failure, and that incomplete answers are acceptable. The reflective process of answering the questions should be highlighted as the purpose, and it should be stated that the specific answers given are not important at this point in the semester. Instead, students would have an opportunity to continue to develop their answers throughout the semester to prepare for their theory of composition. The idea of connection to outside content should also be brought up explicitly. Chris felt that not only would these changes help mitigate anxiety, but would also be instrumental in helping students develop reflective habits conducive to their successful completion of the final project. That is, if students were intentionally trying to connect their answers to these questions to other classes, their teaching, and their other research, they would be able to develop a more robust theory of composition that connected across these contexts. Courtney and Chris felt that the midterm discussion of the questions was the first time they really "got" the content of the course. Having this discussion as early as possible in the semester will probably allow for that epiphany to happen earlier, allowing for transfer to happen more easily earlier in the class.

Another primary change for the curriculum is how "failure" was approached. Part of the design of the class was to allow for "critical incidents" (Yancey, Robertson, and Taczak). In Yancey, Robertson, and Taczak, this is when first-year students recognize how they have been approaching writing assignments will not be effective in college writing. This kind of critical incident can be very positive: it can encourage students to re-evaluate how they perceive knowledge and practices and to reshape new theories. From Ryan's point of view, these struggles were seen as a learning experience in HTC—a way to grow as a student, scholar, and teacher. Colin Brooke and Allison Carr note that these struggles, even failure, "can be an important part of writing development" (62). Trying new things can lead to missteps, and those missteps can be learning experiences. Robert E. Haskell even notes that "fear of failure" may be a disposition of learners that gets in the way of learning transfer (121), especially when students perceive failure as a "lack of talent rather than lack of knowledge, and practice [sic]" (175, quoting John Hayes). From the students' points of view, this "failure" of their theories of composition led to some anxiety. Graduate students are usually used to success (Ebest): they've often done very well in school, and that's why they're in graduate school. Suddenly being put in a position that they perceive themselves as not having the tools necessary to succeed can lead to a lot of anxiety. What Ryan took as a learning experience, some students, including Courtney, Sue, and Chris, perceived as doing poorly in the course, even not being prepared for graduate school.

The idea of failure, its benefit for learning, and how the class allows for safe "failure" should be discussed explicitly early on. Students should be given the opportunity to reflect upon and redevelop theories and practices in a safe way. This could perhaps be done through more peer-to-peer discussions on topics, especially on the larger projects in the class. But this should also be done through more detailed reviews of expectations: discussions of what is expected through reading responses, projects, and presentations. Simply stating that the struggle is positive may allay some of the students' fears by letting them know that the instructor *wants* some struggle. Perhaps even reflections on failure could be advantageous. Allowing students to understand their own relationship with failure and reflecting on positive outcomes of failure could help them view "failure" in the context of the class differently. These direct discussions of failure would allow students to more readily discuss the struggle instead of hiding it. As Chris pointed out, imposter syndrome is common among graduate students, which in his case, led to anxiety about the struggles he faced in recognizing critical incidents for what they were—learning opportunities rather than complete failures.

Discussion in general was a big part of allowing for critical incidents. Students said they were able to come to these moments in a safer way in small group discussion than they were in full-class discussion. They felt this was because the small groups allowed them to realize other students were also struggling. Especially for more difficult topics, discussing in small groups before talking directly to the full class (especially talking to the instructor) might be very helpful. The discussion allows for this type of rethinking of theories to happen in a more private way before the theories are discussed more publicly with the rest of the class. Sue, Courtney, and Chris confirmed that earlier and more frequent peer-to-peer discussions would have significantly aided their comfort-level when wrestling with the material and would have provided them with low-risk opportunities for asking what they perceived as "dumb" questions. Through lower-stakes interactions with peers and, in this case, more advanced students in the program, Sue felt this change would provide greater chance for validation and clarification regarding areas of struggle and "critical incidents."

The final major revision of the curriculum is probably the most difficult: weaving the questions and transfer into the course content in more substantial ways. As stated above, transparency about transfer would help the students understand the reasons behind the curriculum. This also goes for the major projects: why were students doing the Expansion, Context, and Gap projects, for example? What was the outcome for each assignment, and how did that outcome connect to course outcomes? Taking some time to discuss this in class could be helpful for students. In the case of the projects above, students were put in a position to connect class content to content outside of the class, but at the time, the student didn't see that.

It may also be helpful to try to explicitly connect the major projects: how might theories from one of the major projects help with another? How are the projects similar? Different? Getting students to think about the ways the projects relate can help them to get more out of the projects in general, but it can also serve as a smaller-scale opportunity for learning transfer by encouraging them to connect one project to another. Connecting the projects could help build upon learning instead of treating each project as separate. If they can connect projects, they won't be "strangers in strange lands" (McCarthy) every time they begin a new project.

This kind of weaving might also be seen in reading responses and in-class discussions. Connecting *back* to the 11 main class questions regularly in reading response prompts and class discussions could help to keep those questions on students' minds more immediately. While Ryan did attempt to do this in both reading response prompts and class discussions, he did not explicitly remind students of the questions to which he was connecting. That small but important step could help to remind students of the importance of those questions and the importance of connecting to contexts beyond the classroom. For example, pedagogy concerns often came up in class discussion. Ryan thought the connection to the questions on pedagogy from the 11 questions was clear, but most of the students did not immediately think about those questions as part of the discussion. Simply taking that extra step of reminding students of questions 3, 4, and 5 from the list—even restating the questions as part of the discussion—may help students to build theories of their teaching practices instead of just discussing pedagogy devoid of larger pedagogical connections. To this end, David felt that putting these pedagogical questions in conversation with sustained critical self-reflection on his then-current teaching practices, as a regular part of class discussion, would have helped him identify the obstacles he experienced sooner. Moreover, greater discussion of major projects would not only help novice students like Chris to establish more holistic theories of the discipline but could also allow advanced students like David to use these assignments to explore new areas of scholarship, forge new connections, and thus broaden their knowledge of the discipline.

At this point, themes in the revision for the curriculum may seem clear: transparency and connection helped students understand the outcomes of the course more clearly and likely would help them to transfer to contexts outside of the class more easily. While overall, David, Sue, Courtney, and Chris found the curriculum to be helpful, they believed it would be more helpful with revisions that allowed for more explicit explanations and more transparency.

Graduate students are still becoming part of the discourse of rhetoric and composition as they take courses but may at times be expected to already know exactly what they are doing. They are expected to learn the discourse and to synthesize and apply the discourse simultaneous. Of course, this can be quite difficult and may require ample reflection and explicit guidance from graduate instructors. The purpose of this course is to help apprentice them into the discipline more carefully. Transfer theory can certainly help to encourage students to use the theories from graduate classes to enhance their own teaching and research. Instructors of graduate classes can encourage students to mindfully build out their own theories of composition and can help them to become scholars who "guide knowledge making in composition studies" (Marback 824) instead of just taking in what they have learned. In essence, graduate instructors can help to bring graduate students into the discourse of the field more quickly and to get them engaged as productive scholars in composition studies.

While this course is designed specifically for History and Theories of Composition, the lessons about transfer and connection can be applied to other courses in graduate education as well. As a field, composition scholars should attempt to make an effort to build graduate courses that allow for students to build, shape, and reshape their theory of composition.

Works Cited

Anson, Chris M., and Susan K. Miller-Cochran. "Contrails of Learning: Using New Technologies for Vertical Knowledge Building." *Computers and Composition*, vol. 50, 2009, pp. 38-48.

Bergmann, Linda S., and Janet Zepernick. "Disciplinarity and Transfer: Students' Perceptions of Learning to Write." *WPA: Writing Program Administration*, vol. 31, no. 1-2, 2007, pp. 124-149.

Brooke, Colin, and Allison Carr. "Failure Can Be an Important Part of Writing Development." *Naming What We Know: Threshold Concepts of Writing Studies*, edited by Linda Adler-Kassner and Elizabeth Wardle, Utah State University Press, 2015, pp. 62-64.

Dively, Ronda Leathers. "Standardizing English 101 at Southern Illinois University Carbondale: Reflections on Promise of Improved GTA Preparation and More Effective Writing Instruction." *Composition Forum*, vol. 22, 2010, http://compositionforum.com/issue/22/siuc.php. Accessed 22 January 2018.

Downs, Douglas, and Elizabeth Wardle. "Teaching about Writing, Righting Misconceptions: (Re)envisioning 'First-Year Composition' as 'Introduction to Writing Studies.'" *College Composition and Communication,* vol. 58, no. 4, 2007, pp. 552-584.

Driscoll, Dana Lynn, and Jennifer Wells. "Beyond Knowledge and Skills: Writing Transfer and the Role of Student Dispositions." *Composition Forum*, vol. 26, 2012, https://compositionforum.com/issue/26/beyond-knowledge-skills.php. Accessed 30 March 2020.

Driscoll, Dana Lynn, and Roger Powell. "States, Traits, and Dispositions: The Impact of Emotion on Writing Development and Writing Transfer Across College Courses and Beyond." *Composition Forum*, vol. 34, 2016, https://compositionforum.com/issue/34/states-traits.php. Accessed 30 March 2020.

Dryer, Dylan B. "At a Mirror, Darkly: The Imagined Undergraduate Writers of Ten Novice Composition instructors." *College Composition and Communication*, vol. 63, no. 3, 2012, pp. 420-452.

Ebest, Sally Barr. "When Graduate Students Resist." *WPA: Writing Program Administration*, vol. 26, no. 1, 2002, pp. 27-43.

Gere, Anne Ruggles. "Kitchen Tables and Rented Rooms: The Extracurriculum of Composition." *Literacy: A Critical Sourcebook*, edited by Ellen Cushman, Eugene R. Kintgen, Barry M. Kroll, and Mike Rose, Bedford/St. Martin's, 2001, pp. 275-289.

Haskell, Robert E. *Transfer of Learning: Cognition, Instruction, and Reasoning*, Academic Press, 2001.

Khost, Peter H., Debra Rudder Lohe, and Chuck Sweetman. "Rethinking and Unthinking the Graduate Seminar." *Pedagogy*, vol. 15, no. 1, 2014, pp. 19-30.

Mack, Nancy. "Representations of the Field in Graduate Courses: Using Parody to Question All Positions. *College English*, vol. 71, no. 5, 2009, pp. 435-459.

Marback, Richard. "Being Reasonable: A Proposal for Doctoral Education in Composition Studies." *JAC*, vol. 21, no. 4, 2001, pp. 821-839.

McCarthy, Lucille Parkinson. "A Stranger in Strange Lands: A College Student Writing across the Curriculum." *Research in the Teaching of English*, vol. 21, no. 3, 1981, pp. 233-265.

Nelms, Gerald, and Ronda Leathers Dively. "Perceived Roadblocks to Transferring Knowledge from First-Year Composition to Writing Intensive Major Courses: A Pilot Study. *WPA: Writing Program Administration*, vol. 31, no. 1-2, 2007, pp. 214-240.

Nowacek, Rebecca S. *Agents of Integration: Understanding Transfer as a Rhetorical Act*. Southern Illinois University Press, 2011.

Robertson, Liane, Kara Taczak, and Kathleen Blake Yancey. "Notes Toward a Theory of Prior Knowledge and Its Role in College Composers' Transfer of Knowledge and Practice." *Composition Forum*, vol. 26, 2012, http://compositionforum.com/issue/26/prior-knowledge-transfer.php. Accessed 2 Nov 2016.

Salomon, Gavriel, and David N. Perkins. "Rocky Roads to Transfer: Rethinking Mechanism of a Neglected Phenomenon." *Educational Psychologist*, vol. 24, no. 2, 1989, pp. 113-142.

Shepherd, Ryan P. "Digital Writing, Multimodality, and Learning Transfer: Crafting Connections between Composition and Online Composing." *Computers and Composition*, vol. 48, 2018, pp. 103-114.

Stancliff, Michael, and Maureen Daly Goggin. "What's Theorizing Got to Do with It? Teaching Theory as Resourceful Conflict and Reflection in TA Preparation." *WPA: Writing Program Administration*, vol. 30, no. 3, 2007, pp. 11-28.

Taczak, Kara, and Kathleen Blake Yancey. "Threshold Concepts in Rhetoric and Composition Doctoral Education: The Delivered, Lived, and Experienced Curricula." *Naming What We Know: Threshold Concepts of Writing Studies*, edited by Linda Adler-Kassner and Elizabeth Wardle, Utah State University Press, 2015, pp. 140-154.

Yancy, Kathleen Blake, Liane Robertson, and Kara Taczak. *Writing Across Contexts: Transfer, Composition and Sites of Writing*, Utah State University Press, 2014.

Appendix 1: Focal Questions

- How do you define "composition"?
- What (if any) is the relationship between composition studies and English studies?
- How should composition be taught (in the first year and beyond)?
- What are the goals of composition (first-year writing and other contexts)?
- How can and should these goals be met?
- How should composition be studied? Why?
- What are the goals of composition research?
- What methodologies can best lead us to those goals?
- What ties us together as a discipline?
- What do you see as the central "threshold concepts"?
- How do these concepts inform your teaching and research?

English 391ml: Multilingualism and Literacy in Western Mass

Rebecca Lorimer Leonard, Kyle Piscioniere, Danielle Pappo

Course Description

College students continue to navigate powerful literacy myths that impact their writing education, especially the belief systems that uphold standard, monolingual uses of language (Shapiro and Watson; Watson). The course we describe here, "English 391ml: Multilingualism and Literacy in Western Mass," raises students' critical awareness of language by engaging them in the lived experience of writing among languages. This course combines several strands of innovation in composition studies: an upper-division writing-about-writing (WAW) course, a WAW course focused on multilingual writing, and a community literacy partnership with a local language school that serves immigrants and international students.

English 391ml is an upper-division elective that introduces undergraduates to literacy studies through the lens of language diversity, examining what literacy and multilingualism mean in theory and in the communities surrounding the University of Massachusetts, Amherst.[1] Taught by Rebecca Lorimer Leonard with assistance from graduate students Danielle Pappo and Kyle Piscioniere, English 391ml asks students to make meaning not only *through* literacy but also *of* literacy, exploring the social significance of literacy in all of its routines, values, and belief systems (Brandt). By thinking across classroom and community contexts, students especially encounter the tension between academic theories (for example, English as hegemonic global language) and urgent expressed community needs (English as workplace necessity). English 391ml aims to be functional, providing writing support for a local school and community experience for UMass students, but also important, complicating commonplace assumptions about literacy's problems and promises for all participants.

Institutional Context

The University of Massachusetts Amherst is the flagship of the University of Massachusetts system. Founded in 1863 as a land-grant agricultural school, "Mass Aggie" evolved into Massachusetts State College in 1931 to reflect its broadening curriculum. Soon afterward it became the University of Mas-

---

1. You can find the syllabi and course calendars for each Course Design essay on the *Composition Studies* website at https://compstudiesjournal.com/.

sachusetts, a major research university with a current student population of 28,000 and commitments to the liberal arts, STEM, numerous professional schools, and community outreach ("Our History"). English 391ml is a designated service learning course and fulfills a requirement for UMass' interdisciplinary Certificate in Civic Engagement & Public Service. In addition to English majors, the course has drawn majors from biology, economics, education, linguistics, political science, psychology, Spanish, and theater and attracted students with a more diverse language background than is the UMass norm, with nearly half of students identifying as multilingual or fluent in a language other than English.

The UMass Amherst English Department has a diverse 43-member faculty teaching primarily literature but also in areas such as American studies, creative writing, and composition and rhetoric. English 391ml is an upper-division elective for the English major and counts for the undergraduate specialization in the study and practice of writing (SPOW), which offers undergraduate courses in composition and rhetoric. English 391ml's course content, from the fields of composition, literacy, education, and TESOL, remains unusual to most of the course's English majors and to all of the students from outside the department. Thus, students react to the course as a rare find, and evaluations show their requests for more courses like this in the department.

The course's community partner, the International Language Institute of Western Massachusetts (ILI), is a non-profit community language school in Northampton whose mission is to promote intercultural understanding and strong, diverse communities through language instruction and teacher training. ILI runs a variety of programs using a two-part funding model wherein they offer TESOL certification and world language courses to fund free English programs for immigrants and refugees. ILI is well known and highly respected in the local area, but as a nonprofit community organization, it remains subject to unreliable funding streams. Therefore, the years-long relationship between Rebecca Lorimer Leonard and ILI's Executive Director Caroline Gear aims for mutually productive symbiosis in English 391ml's community writing projects.

Theoretical Rationale

English 391ml's content, structure, and activities are informed by a theoretical framework at the intersection of sociocultural approaches to literacy (Gee; Street), post-structural approaches to language diversity (Canagarajah; Garcia; Makoni and Pennycook; You), and critical approaches to community engagement (Crookes; Mitchell; Rice and Pollack; Rosenberger). This theoretical framework is designed to prepare students for the instability of the course's two operational terms—literacy and multilingualism—as students encounter them in community settings. For good reason, community members often want and need the cognitive and economic promises that cling to literacy and the English language, even if such promises are "debunked" in scholarship. Thus, UMass students experience a multi-stage unveiling of course content: first, that literacy and language are always social and rarely stable (students are surprised); second, that neither theoretical notion is easily legible in settings where multilingual literacies are lived (students are humbled); and third, that community definitions of literacy and language are as true as academic ones, and that these truths can co-exist.

This inevitable (and planned) student experience of dissonance equips students to grapple with the "unquestioned belief systems" around literacy and multilingualism that are in wide circulation (Watson 165). The course frequently revisits the observation that although composition has deepened its concepts of literacy, it often does so at the expense of literacy as it is lived (Brandt 460). In readings, discussions, assigned and informal writing, and community projects, English 391ml students are asked not to reconcile these tensions but to look at them as their family members would, and as their community partners must.

Course Content and Structure

Course reading includes scholarly pieces introducing students to transnational and multilingual writing (Lam and Rosario-Ramos; Lippi-Green; Lorimer Leonard; Marko), and critical approaches to community literacy (Auerbach et al.; Perry). Students begin with Deborah Brandt and James Paul Gee to become conversant in approaches to literacy as made up of "words, deeds, and things" (Gee), and then approach literacy as a site of power (Freire; Scribner) that is simultaneously subjugatory and liberatory (Brandt and Clinton).

This groundwork prepares students to discuss three focal ethnographies that examine multilingual literacies in diverse and often troubling contexts. Students rely on the essential premise of each study, that literacy is socio-material matter "coursing through institutions, places, and history," to explore ethnographic narratives of multilingualism as it is lived (Vieira 4). Each offers a different angle on literacy's ideologies: Tomás Mario Kalmar's *Illegal Alphabets* demonstrates an asset-based approach to emergent bilingualism, showing that bilingual migrants are already and uniquely equipped with the means for collaboratively and creatively self-educating; Kate Vieira's *American by Paper* clarifies the tangibly hard material of immigrants' literacies: the borders, papers, and money they navigate as their national status fluctuates; Catherine Prendergast's *Buying into English* reveals the ethnic, economic, political components that allow English language literacies to count only sometimes and only for some. Each book exposes the careful balancing act of its subjects' hope and fear, liberation and subordination, desires, imaginaries, and realities. At each turn, the three books are animated by and invigorate the course's writing activities and community engagement in important ways.

For example, the writing projects chosen by the community partner impact what students see in their course reading. In the course's first semester, when ILI asked UMass students to develop a curriculum to help their immigrant students earn driver's licenses, UMass students noticed that driving was a powerful theme across the ethnographies. In discussion, they traced the literate activities and knowledge demanded by being in a car in the U.S.: the migrants in *Illegal Alphabets* initiate their literacy learning after the hit-and-run death of a fellow farmworker. Driver's licenses are powerful materials that "promote and constrain movement" among Azorean and Brazilian communities in *American by Paper*. In *Buying into English*, the commodification of English is symbolized in luxury cars that carry (empty) promises for language learners. In each study, driving is a sign, symptom, and response to communities' access to literacy. Therefore, as students designed the ILI driving curriculum, their conversations were informed by vivid ethnographic depictions of literacy's interconnected opportunities and constraints. As the driving curriculum evolved over multiple semesters, students revised its content and structure to 1) recognize the material and social "rhetorical blockages" ILI students might encounter on the road (Marko et al.), and 2) negotiate and transform those blockages with a curriculum based in storytelling and locally collected narratives.

Writing Assignments and Activities

In this way, all course writing leads students to challenge and extend the literacy and language theories they read. This happens in several categories of writing activities: eight 250-word informal reflections; three formal 4-6 page analyses; and a community project of their choice.

Following the centrality of reflection writing in much community engaged pedagogy, students compose informal reflections throughout the semester to respond to course reading or community experiences. Students have used these reflections to articulate their personal response to course readings; synthesize the reading's claims or concepts; make connections between reading and their own life, the lives they engage with at ILI, or lives they see represented in media; and generally lay the developmental groundwork for their formal writing assignments. Students post reflections on the course management site, and Rebecca Lorimer Leonard synthesizes and echoes back their major points in class to begin discussion. Course evaluations point to the low-stakes nature of the reflections as an essential space for students to work out the complexities not only of the readings but of the way the readings conflict with what they see in their community work.

The first formal assignment is an analysis of the concept of literacy, which students write prior to beginning their community project. The paper asks students to develop a scholarly definition of literacy based on course reading and then analyze that definition in one context of their choosing: in an ongoing news story about immigration, in their own family (as gathered through a family literacy history interview), or on the website of a literacy organization. To practice this analytic genre once again, the second paper asks students to apply their developing definition of literacy to one community experience. The paper aims to facilitate students' continued negotiation of the desires and needs of the community site in light of the hierarchies of multilingual literacies. The final writing assignment for the course asks students to articulate a philosophy of literacy that reflects upon their position among the competing social and academic understandings of literacy explored in the course. Akin to Kathleen Blake Yancey, Liane Robertson, and Kara Taczak's personal "theory of writing," the assignment gives students an opportunity to fully explore their values and beliefs around literacy and multilingualism and show how those values are supported with examples from their writing, thinking, and community work over the course of the semester (110).

Community Writing and Activities

A month into the semester, students begin working at ILI alongside the ILI's students, teachers, and staff. Community activities have so far included four projects, all proposed by ILI: 1) an editorial revision of ILI's host family guidebook; 2) individual, long-term tutoring for immigrants taking courses in ILI's free evening English program (FEEP); 3) developing a driving curriculum for ILI students who need to get their driver's licenses in the U.S. (supporting the literacies needed to take the online and road test); and 4) a weekly pop-up writing center to support the academic writing of ILI's international students studying in their Intensive English Program (IEP). The two tutoring projects are distinct in population, content, and timing. With FEEP, tutors support immigrants and refugees with a wide range of language and literacy levels while the pop-up writing center tutors work with the IEP's students and scholars; the content for FEEP students is primarily English conversation, while the IEP students ask for support in academic writing; and FEEP tutors commit to at least one year in order to develop long-term relationships, while IEP tutors support students depending on enrollment session. So, the FEEP tutoring is designed to be sustained and based in long-term relationships, while the pop-up writing center is designed to respond to the IEP's always-shifting needs with spatial and chronological flexibility.

All of these activities are guided by Gerald Campano, Maria Paula Ghiso, and Bethany J. Welch's "coalitional" approach to community literacy whereby project members are reflective with respect to social location and aim to build coalitional energy at the community site, investigate and center community members' experiences, and work toward a shared vision of social change. Thus, the second half of the semester pushes students to consider why they signed up to offer "service" to multilingual immigrants in the first place. Students read Keith Morton's "Paradigms of Service Learning" to articulate their own service values and Auerbach et al.'s guidebook on participatory learning, *From the Community to the Community*, as a model of community literacy that decenters universities as the locus of expertise.

To find expertise in lived experience and cultivate it there is to begin *elsewhere* than students often imagine. Thus, throughout their community collaboration, students cycle through reflection/action, education/identification, provocation/reaction, and distance/closeness, each necessarily shaped through emotion. These cycles are supported by the course structure and prompted by formal and informal writing: at least half of reflection posts and formal assignments begin by asking students to identify a "personal concern," anguish, anger, or grief, in pursuit of public action and deeper learning (Marko et al. 20). The feelings of others, too—in course readings, among the lives of students, and students and staff at the ILI—are revealed not as mere instances but as indicators of social and structural positioning, emotion as embedded in the work of community engagement and activism more broadly.

While the stated goals of English 391ml include guiding students, teachers, and community members to reflect on their relationship to literacy and grapple with persistent myths about monolingualism, multilingualism, and the English language, feedback from all project participants has shown that other surprising learning outcomes have resulted from the activities above. For example, UMass students and ILI staff, after discussing Auerbach et al.'s and Marko et al.'s projects, question the social and political disconnects between academic and community versions of literacy practice and research. UMass students express continual pleasure that ethnographic narrative accounts count as meaningful support for academic arguments. And project leaders, including the authors of this article as well as ILI staff, are often surprised how the course draws out the multilingual life experiences and skills of a UMass student population often assumed to be monolingual. English 391ml students, throughout a semester of writing and discussing their own literate repertoires and those of their families and community partners, show themselves to be composing from highly diverse language repertoires, shaped by their multilingual immigrant families; their personal language pursuits for travel, work, or self-enrichment; or the multilingual communities they participate in online.

Critical Reflection

Two characteristics of English 391ml have emerged as potentially interesting for composition studies. First, the course destabilizes the relationship between academic, personal, and community knowledge by exploring the legitimacy of language and literacy hierarchies (Lippi-Green). Second, the course's community partnership foregrounds relationships as one basis of democratic participation.

Language and Literacy Hierarchies

English 391ml leads students to question what counts as literacy and language knowledge and who counts as knowledgeable language users. Students experience their community work as a validity check for academic readings and thinking; at the same time, their academic theory sculpts their community work with critical lenses on service learning and language ideology. The results are not only intellectually rigorous, but rooted in generous, empathetic thinking grown from personal connection. For example, after reading Rosina Lippi-Green's section on the "Standard Language Myth," students analyze how standard language ideology circulates in the community partner site. One student observed in a reflection that ILI deployed standard language ideology pragmatically, not "because it believes that there is one standard form of English…but rather because it aims to equip students with the language skills that have been found necessary to succeed in a society that focuses on the use of one standard English." Firsthand relationships with the community partner steer students away from bad faith criticism. Instead, they investigate how standard language might be combatted, ethically or strategically deployed, and how its omnipresence seeps into even the most progressive missions.

Building on these firsthand relationships at ILI, students explicitly rethink the sites of knowledge production. In the words of one student, collaboration with ILI helps blur "seemingly arbitrary bureaucratic borders" to resituate "which academic spaces are 'real' or 'not real.'" Research sheds some of its aloof authority. Students bridge connections from classroom knowledge to personal knowledge, rethinking their home literacies and coming to see themselves as research instruments. Following course readings that carefully attend to the people whose literacies are studied, students build their literacy knowledge laterally, communally, and reciprocally. Students carry this active knowledge-building into their writing and thinking, especially when composing their literacy philosophy, which asks them to imagine a model of literacy that bridges emotionally resonant personal experiences and robust academic inquiry.

This line of questioning also leads students to reconsider the university's responsibilities and obligations. In one class conversation, a pre-med student vented about the lack of opportunities for STEM students to learn through community engagement, let alone critically reflect on the impulse to serve others. Another student responded with visions of what a community-engaged university should prioritize, both in its mission and activities. By the end of English 391ml, students begin to imagine not just what the university could do next, but what the university might next come to be.

Relationships as Democratic Participation

The course's community work also fosters collaborative composition as a means of democratic action imbued with the acts of listening, understanding, and writing. During one pop-up writing center session, a group of ILI students—from across the world, with literacies emerging from such diverse experiences as motherhood, PhD programs, poetry, and international NGO work—were tasked with writing an essay about local Western Massachusetts politics. The instructor asked the UMass tutors if ILI students could interview them for a "local's perspective" on local issues. The conversations that followed became a site of reflection and analysis for the rest of the semester.

The activity demanded a rethinking of UMass and ILI student subjectivities. UMass students initially felt uncomfortable being called "locals." In fact, UMass students felt distinctly un-local, despite growing up in New England. Their temporary status in Western Mass clashed with the ILI students' status as new, but in some cases hopefully permanent, members of the Northampton community. The negotiation over the term "local" was not just a semantic argument. It was the mapping of a community relationship, read as a question of writing methodology and civic governance. As participants and students shared their experiences, they began the messy work of thinking across axes of difference to explore complex political questions. The process was not designed to *solve* those political questions. Rather, participants sought to write about them: ILI students for their papers on American politics, UMass students for their literacy philosophies.

That testing of the term "local" is representative of the course's restorative political frame; that the term was tested in service to a writing assignment is representative of literacy's primacy to this frame. The course takes up calls by Nancy Welch, Steve Parks, Mary Ann Cain, and others to foster community-based, civic participation in classrooms. But the course's model of civic action is not rooted in agonistic rhetoric, the public circulation of texts, or deliberative consensus-building. While contemporary conversations around national politics can stray easily into despair, the course instead offers a viable model of democratic engagement that goes beyond lament or critique. At ILI, the functions of the state, while always present, recede. The forging of relationships, the immediate focus on a *task at hand* emerges as a powerful and restorative engagement with the ethos of democracy. That English 391ml invites students to explore engagement in this mode feels especially meaningful in our moment of foreclosed politics, when students recognize the call to political action but face a multi-decade neoliberal assault on the channels of their participation (Fox and Eidman-Aadahl; Welch 13).

Course Challenges and Future Revisions

Even with these strengths, English 391ml can benefit from pushing the critical capacity of all participants' learning as the course and its relationship with ILI evolves. For example, the focus of course content demands that the instructor pay careful attention to students' full literacy repertoires. Because both university and community students bring full literacy lives to the partnership, which are then examined and complicated as the course content, future iterations of English 391ml could build in earlier and more intentional discussion and assignment space to draw out students' language backgrounds and goals, especially when they enter the partnership with anachronistic beliefs surrounding literacy, multilingualism, and service initiatives.

There also is room to further develop their critical understanding of language ideologies, particularly in terms of existing theories of critical literacy (Janks) or critical language awareness (Fairclough). By incorporating readings on literacy from applied linguistics or social justice education, students would be exposed to scholarly conversations relevant to their community collaborations and not always taught to undergraduates in English departments. In this way, the course reading list should continue to evolve based on the community partner and adapt to the nature of each proposed community project. For instance, Prendergast's *Buying into English* gave pop-up writing center tutors necessary examples of transnational language ideologies that shaped ILI students' acquisition of academic English, helping UMass tutors navigate those ideologies alongside ILI students. Similarly, Tamera Marko et al.'s "Proyecto Carrito" offered English 391ml students who were working on the driving curriculum another way to connect the act of driving to literacy and activism. As future community projects or partners shift so will the course reading need to shift in turn. In other words, the course structure and rationale can stay constant as community partners or needs evolve, while the content will need to remain flexible for the most responsive version of the course.

Further, the number and type of community projects may need to change in pursuit of a more focused UMass/ILI relationship. So far, UMass students have worked in small groups, some to tutor, some to work on curriculum, some to redesign ILI materials. However, future versions of the course may consolidate projects to give students a more common touchstone and to accomplish fewer but more quickly completed projects. As is well-charted by

Elsa Auerbach, Thomas Deans, Morton and many other community engaged scholars, community engaged courses provide rigorous and unpredictable instructional experiences. All participants must balance a suite of expectations in light of project timelines that may stretch or shrink depending on student interest or community partner communication. To maintain sustainability in the partnership, Rebecca Lorimer Leonard has used the flexibility of independent studies (sometimes leading six at a time) to keep students involved beyond the confines of a one-semester course. Therefore, the future of each project, like the pop-up writing center, also will be subject to future funding and administrative interest as Rebecca Lorimer Leonard's teaching duties shift.

Finally, the course's spatial split between community and classroom can lead to the perennial shorthand between the community "out there" and the class "in here." Such in/out mentality risks positioning the community partner as a group to be studied, rather than to be collaboratively joined in pursuit of common questions. Perhaps UMass students should meet only at the community site and only alongside their community partners. At its best the course provides all students new critical frames to "drive their own narrative" about literacy and multilingualism (Marko et al. 32). Optimally, future versions of the course will help drive these narratives into further social change.

Works Cited

Auerbach, Elsa, Byron Barahona, Julio Midy, Felipe Vaquerano, and Ana Zambranol. *Adult ESL/literacy from the Community to the Community: A Guidebook for Participatory Literacy Training.* Routledge, 2013.

Brandt, Deborah. "Remembering Writing, Remembering Reading." *College Composition and Communication*, vol. 45, no. 4, 1994, pp. 459–479.

Brandt, Deborah, and Katie Clinton. "Limits of the Local: Expanding Perspectives on Literacy as a Social Practice." *Journal of Literacy Research*, vol. 34, no. 3, 2002, pp. 337-356.

Campano, Gerald, María Paula Ghiso, and Bethany J. Welch. *Partnering with Immigrant Communities: Action through Literacy.* Teachers College Press, 2016.

Canagarajah, Suresh. *Translingual Practice: Global Englishes and Cosmopolitan Relations.* Routledge, 2012.

Crookes, Graham V. *Critical ELT in Action: Foundations, Promises, Praxis.* Routledge, 2013.

Deans, Thomas. *Writing and Community Action: A Service-learning Rhetoric with Readings.* Longman Publishing Group, 2002.

Fox, Tom and Elyse Eidman-Aadahl. "The National Writing Project in the Age of Austerity." *Composition in the Age of Austerity*, edited by Nancy Welch and Tony Scott, Utah State University Press, 2016, pp. 77-91.

García, Ofelia. *Bilingual Education in the 21st Century: A Global Perspective.* Wiley-Blackwell Publishers, 2009.

Gee, James P. *Social Linguistics and Literacies: Ideology in Discourses.* Routledge, 2012.

Kalmar, Tomás Mario. *Illegal Alphabets and Adult Biliteracy: Latino Migrants Crossing the Linguistic Border.* 2nd ed. Routledge, 2015.

Lam, Wan Shun Eva, and Enid Rosario-Ramos. "Multilingual Literacies in Transnational Digitally Mediated Contexts: An Exploratory Study of Immigrant Teens in the United States." *Language and Education*, vol. 23, no. 2, 2009, pp. 171-190.

Lippi-Green, Rosina. *English With an Accent: Language, Ideology, and Discrimination in the United States.* 2nd ed., Routledge, 2012.

Lorimer Leonard, Rebecca. "Multilingual Writing as Rhetorical Attunement." *College English*, vol. 76, no. 3, 2014, pp. 227-247.

Makoni, Sinfree, and Alastair Pennycook, editors. *Disinventing and Reconstituting Languages.* Multilingual Matters, 2006.

Marko, Tamera, Mario Ernesto Osorio, Eric Sepenoski, and Ryan Catalani. "Proyecto Carrito—When the Student Receives an 'A' and the Worker Gets Fired: Disrupting the Unequal Political Economy of Translingual Rhetorical Mobility." *Literacy in Composition Studies* vol. 3, no. 1, 2015, pp. 21-43.

Mitchell, Tania D. "Traditional vs. Critical Service-Learning: Engaging the Literature to Differentiate Two Models." *Journal of Community Service Learning*, vol. 14, 2008, pp. 50-65.

Morton, Keith. "The Irony of Service: Charity, Project, and Social Change in Service-Learning." *Michigan Journal of Community Service Learning*, 1995, pp. 19-32.

"Our History: UMass Amherst 150 Years." UMass Amherst, www.umass.edu/150/our-history.

Perry, Kristen H. "Becoming Qualified to Teach Low-literate Refugees: A Case Study of One Volunteer Instructor." *Community Literacy Journal*, v7 n2, 2013, pp. 21-38.

Prendergast, Catherine. *Buying into English: Language and Investment in the New Capitalist World.* University of Pittsburgh Press, 2008.

Rice, Kathleen., and Pollack, Seth "Developing a Critical Pedagogy of Service Learning: Preparing Self-reflective, Culturally Aware, and Responsive Community Participants." *Integrating Service Learning and Multicultural Education in Colleges and Universities*, edited by Carolyn R. O'Grady. Lawrence Erlbaum Associates Publishers, 2000, pp. 115-134.

Rosenberger, Cynthia. "Beyond Empathy: Developing Critical Consciousness through Service Learning. *Integrating Service Learning and Multicultural Education in Colleges and Universities*, edited by Carolyn R. O'Grady. Lawrence Erlbaum Associates Publishers, 2000, pp. 23-43.

Scribner, Sylvia. "Literacy in Three Metaphors." *American Journal of Education*, Volume 93, No. 1. Nov. 1984.

Sheridan, David Michael, Jim Ridolfo, and Anthony J. Michel. *The Available Means of Persuasion: Mapping a Theory and Pedagogy of Multimodal Public Rhetoric.* Anderson, SC: Parlor Press, 2012.

Street, Brian. *Social Literacies: Critical Approaches to Literacy in Ethnography, Education, and Development.* Longman, 1995.

Vieira, Kate. *American by Paper: How Documents Matter in Immigrant Literacy.* University of Minnesota Press, 2016.

Watson, Missy. "Contesting Standardized English." *Academe*, May-June 2018.

Watson, Missy, and Rachael Shapiro. "Clarifying the Multiple Dimensions of Monolingualism: Keeping Our Sights on Language Politics." *Composition Forum*, vol. 38, 2018.

Welch, Nancy and Tony Fox. "Introduction: Composition in the Age of Austerity." *Composition in the Age of Austerity*. Utah State University Press, 2016.

Yancey, Kathleen Blake, Laine Robertson, and Kara Taczak. *Writing across Contexts: Transfer, Composition, and Sites of Writing*. University Press of Colorado, 2014.

You, Xiaoye. *Cosmopolitan English and Transliteracy*. Southern Illinois University Press, 2016.

Where We Are

Networking Undergraduate Research: Where We Are, Where We Can Go

Dominic DelliCarpini and Jessie L. Moore

Knowing where we *are* in undergraduate research (UR) in writing studies requires knowing where we *have been*—and how we got here. In retrospect, this development looks less like something planned by an architect and more like the evolutionary fits and starts of multiple invested residents (far more than we can name in this short piece) responding to environmental needs.

Making UR Public

UR in our field became more public when Candace Spiegelman and Laurie Grobman launched *Young Scholars in Writing* in 2003, providing space for the products of emerging writing studies researchers. Presentation and publication venues have grown exponentially, adding venues such as *Xchanges* (est. 2001), *The Pulse* (now *Inquiries*, est. 2009), and *The Jump* (now Jump+, est. 2010).

Seeing the potential of this work, CCCC leaders established the CCCC Committee on Undergraduate Research (5CUR) in 2011 to survey members about UR and to author the *CCCC Position Statement on Undergraduate Research in Writing: Principles and Best Practices* (2017) and its accompanying annotated bibliography (added October 2018). In 2017, the Executive Committee granted 5CUR Special Committee status, allowing it to be reconstituted annually to implement the CCCC Undergraduate Researcher Poster Session, collect and circulate research about UR in the field, and coordinate with the broader UR community. 5CUR supports research-informed, mentored UR and equips CCCC members with public-facing resources for making evidence-based arguments for tangible support for UR at their institutions.

While serving on the CCCC Executive Committee, Jessie pitched a proposal for an Undergraduate Researcher Poster Session (see http://www.writingfaculty.net/undergraduateresearch/) to 2012 Program Chair Chris Anson. UR schedules often do not align with the regular CCCC proposal deadline, so Jessie proposed a later review process for UR posters. A planning team advertised the call for proposals, reviewed submissions, coached accepted presenters' poster development, and created resources for undergraduates navigating the convention. Chris scheduled the poster session adjacent to the 2012 opening session, ensuring strong attendance in support of the undergraduate presenters. Subsequent program chairs offered similar support, and the planning team quickly evolved to include former presenters and other students.

The CCCC SIG, which has met since 2013, functions as another community of practice for UR mentors and UR presenters. While the SIG meeting occasionally features research projects, it more often serves as a gathering space to share UR initiatives, including national efforts like the poster session and the Naylor Workshop, as well as projects at attendees' institutions.

Naming *How* We Know: From Product to Process

Another serendipitous moment came in 2013. Provided with an endowment funded by Irvin S. Naylor to support the work of writing studies, Dominic faced a question: what needs still existed in the matrix of rapidly-evolving work in undergraduate research? Answering this question required an environmental scan similar to the one provided in this essay.

Dominic saw that publication and presentation venues had highlighted the work products of undergraduate researchers. But, as Dominic and Cindy Crimmins noted in their 2010 chapter in *Undergraduate Research in English Studies*, while students in their Teaching and Tutoring Writing course were becoming increasingly interested in the research *topics* of our discipline, they had little experience with our research *methods,* for the reasons articulated by Laurie Grobman and Joyce Kinkead in the same collection:

> Our suspicion is that we as faculty have not articulated to our students the methodology of inquiry in our fields. . . Though the scientific method is transparent, this is not always the case in the humanities. We may not always agree on a process of inquiry; some might even call the discipline fragmented. (Grobman and Kinkead x)

Undergraduate researchers, who had new opportunities to present and publish their work, had fewer opportunities to engage with the methods of our field, except through the heroic—and often unrecognized—work of their faculty mentors. But, frankly, it was more than that. Even with seven full-time faculty in York College of Pennsylvania's Writing program, for example, mentoring that accounted for the rich array of methods that exist in our field was not possible. Both students and faculty members needed help. So, Dominic, Cindy, and one of their trail-blazing undergraduate researchers, Megan Schoettler, decided that the space they could best occupy was finding ways to name *how* we know—to offer students, and their mentors, a way to learn research methods that support the rich fields of inquiry of our discipline. Impressed by the work of the Elon Research Seminars and the Dartmouth Summer Seminar—which brought together scholars to learn from one another—they built a workshop that would do similar work for undergraduate researchers. In effect, they sought to back-fill the gap that Grobman and Kinkead had identified, to help undergraduate researchers learn from a larger group of mentors and create their own community of researchers within our discipline.

Launched in 2014, with the help of generous scholar/mentors, this workshop has been attended by over 140 undergraduates from 39 states, three countries, and 45 different institutions, as well as about 20-25 scholars each year—who have also learned a great deal from each other. Then, in 2018, a group of 43 scholars gathered for the Naylor Symposium to assess the state of UR in our discipline and to make recommendations for its future. The result was *The Naylor Report on Undergraduate Research in Writing Studies* (2020).

During this period, although not focused specifically on UR in writing studies, the 2014-2016 research seminar on Excellence in Mentored Undergraduate Research, hosted by the Center for Engaged Learning at Elon University, and Council on Undergraduate Research (CUR) conferences and publications also shaped practices in our field by advancing scholarship on mentored UR.

In 2016, Joyce Kinkead published *Researching Writing: An Introduction to Research Methods* to teach undergraduates "how to conduct ethical, authentic research" in writing studies by introducing a "range of methodological approaches—both humanistic and social scientific" to the discipline's novices (xvii-xviii). It also outlines course frameworks that can help professors build authentic projects for students within the context of a class. Likewise, Lauren Fitzgerald and Melissa Ianetta included in *The Oxford Guide for Writing Tutors: Practice and Research* (2015) chapters on research methods that help writing center tutors generate research projects based upon both their lived experiences and the field's methods.

While this short piece cannot chronicle all the efforts of countless thoughtful scholar/mentors who have fueled this movement, these moments demonstrate how key work synergistically provides a future for the continued growth of UR in our discipline. So what's next?

Next Steps: Networking to Connect

UR in writing studies has grown naturally *from* needs, and *through* a combination of commitment and serendipity. Although individual people, events, and publications have moved this work forward, they often operated in distinct orbits with minimal coordination. As we look forward, the next natural need may be greater synergy– or, in the spirit of Kristie Fleckenstein, Clay Spinuzzi, Rebecca Rickly, and Carol Clark Papper's (2008) ecological metaphor, "harmony." As such, we challenge the field to imagine what might be possible with more networking among these efforts. As 5CUR takes ownership of the annual poster session, for example, how might SIG members and other UR mentors collaborate with 5CUR to invite additional participation by Naylor scholars and other students? How might access to the benefits of UR in our field be widened to include more underrepresented groups? How might networking scaffold students' development of publications based on their presentations? And how might building on the national network of Naylor mentors facilitate a community of practice that extends beyond place-based events like the Naylor Workshop and the CCCC SIG? Looking back on nearly 20 years of professionalization of UR in writing studies, we are optimistic that the field's capacity for networking will expand access to and enrich the quality of mentored UR for our next generation of colleagues.

Works Cited

CCCC. *Position Statement on Undergraduate Research in Writing: Principles and Best Practices*, 2017, https://cccc.ncte.org/cccc/resources/positions/undergraduate-research

DelliCarpini, Dominic, and Cindy Crimmins. "The Writing Center as a Space for Undergraduate Research." *Undergraduate Research in English Studies*, edited by Laurie Grobman and Joyce Kinkead, NCTE, 2010, pp. 191-211.

DelliCarpini, Dominic, Jenn Fishman, and Jane Greer. *The Naylor Report on Undergraduate Research in Writing Studies*. Parlor P, 2020.

Fitzgerald, Lauren, and Melissa Ianetta. *The Oxford Guide for Writing Tutors: Practice and Research*. Oxford UP, 2015.

Fleckenstein, Kristie S., et al. "The Importance of Harmony: An Ecological Metaphor for Writing Research." *College Composition and Communication*, vol. 60, no. 2, 2008, pp. 388–419.

Grobman, Laurie, and Joyce Kinkead. "Introduction: Illuminating Undergraduate Research in English." *Undergraduate Research in English Studies*, edited by Laurie Grobman and Joyce Kinkead, NCTE, 2010, pp. ix-xxxii.

Kinkead, Joyce. *Researching Writing: An Introduction to Research Methods*. Utah State UP, 2016.

Theorizing with Undergraduate Researchers

Kristine Johnson and J. Michael Rifenburg

If this section of *Composition Studies* and increasing interest in the field are any indication, composition studies—the field of writing studies—is in a good place. Our field creates space for undergraduate research at its major conferences, events such as the Naylor Workshop for Undergraduate Research in Writing Studies bring together students and faculty from across the country, and writing centers have long been a natural venue for fostering undergraduate research. In our work, we are also seeing more attention to the ways in which undergraduate research can be more accessible, particularly as the demographics of higher education change. Undergraduate research *is* possible for underrepresented and adult students to conduct and for contingent faculty members to mentor. With creative, thoughtful administrative support, it is possible to create cultures of undergraduate research, to involve graduate students as mentors, and to value this work in the tenure and promotion process. Where we are is good, and we have reasons to be hopeful for the future—reasons to hope that undergraduate research in writing studies can be an intellectually and personally meaningful part of college for more and more students.

As we move forward, we call the field to take seriously student voices in the project of theorizing undergraduate research. One obstacle to this call is our strong attachment to student writers and student writing. Student writing functions as a key object of inquiry in the field, and it often serves as evidence of *our* pedagogical agency and *our* theories of writing. Although she endorses the idea that published, peer-reviewed undergraduate research is scholarship, Amy Robillard confesses what many feel: her initial "professional impulse on citing the work of Bastian and Harkness [undergraduate researchers] is to analyze their work as student writing, to draw on it as support for a pedagogical argument" (256). Viewing the products of undergraduate research as scholarly contributions to the field requires a shift in both category and perspective. Undergraduate research cannot be categorized as *student writing* and thus evidence of our pedagogical agency. It must instead be categorized as scholarship and thus evidence of student intellectual agency.

Publishing undergraduate research is critical, but undergraduate student voices must be present in scholarship *about* undergraduate research. Undergraduate researchers should participate in discussions about mentoring practices and accessibility, and frankly, they should be given the opportunity to respond to our representations of them (undergraduate researchers) and their work (undergraduate research). In the call for proposals for our special issue of *Pedagogy* (2021) on undergraduate research in English studies, we asked students and faculty to write together about their research experiences. And in doing so, we believed we had good aims. We wanted students and faculty to tell their stories together in part because undergraduate research is mentored, collaborative research. And for entirely practical purposes, we wanted a faculty member involved in what will be a two-year long publication process. When we received these stories about undergraduate research, we learned a great deal: we learned how the whiteness of the field influences research experiences, how socioeconomic status influences the choices students make about publishing their work, and how faculty and students work in and around institutional realities. Yet in our desire to incorporate student voices, we also fell into a familiar trap and allowed students voices to exist only alongside faculty voices—to narrate the undergraduate research experience but not to critique or theorize it. We wonder what we would have learned by asking students to respond to scholarship about them and about the future of undergraduate research.

Where we are is good, but where we are neglects the student perspective and constrains student agency. To expand our myopic perspective, we suggest looking outside of our discipline, especially to colleagues in the Scholarship of Teaching and Learning. For example, the Students as Partners (SaP) approach defines the student–faculty partnership as "a reciprocal process through which all participants have the opportunity to contribute equally, although not necessarily in the same ways, to curricular or pedagogical conceptualization, decision-making, implementation, investigation, or analysis" (Cook-Sather, Bovill, and Felten 6–7). The SaP principles of respect, reciprocity, and shared responsibility can help us build frameworks for bringing student voices fully and consequentially into scholarship on undergraduate research. Where we are is good. Listening to stories of the work is good. But ensuring that undergraduates talk back is our next imperative.

Works Cited

Cook-Sather, Alison, Catherine Bovill, and Peter Felten. *Engaging Students as Partners in Learning and Teaching: A Guide for Faculty.* Jossey-Bass, 2014.

Robillard, Amy E. "'Young Scholars' Affecting Composition: A Challenge to Disciplinary Citation Practices." *College English,* vol. 68, no. 3, 2006, pp. 253–70.

Inexperience and Innovation

Courtney Buck, Emily Nolan, and Jamie Spallino

Wittenberg University

In the summer that preceded our first semester at Wittenberg University, when questioned about our decision to commit to an intensive research program in a field we knew absolutely nothing about, the three of us likely gave the same robotic answer: "It is a wonderful opportunity." We knew that we were paired with a faculty mentor to work collaboratively on a research project during our first year, and we knew that we'd been presented with a project intended to study the effectiveness of eTutoring comments in Wittenberg University's Writing Center. And that was it. At the time, we had no idea just how true the statement about opportunity really was. Almost two full years later, it's amazing to look back on what we've accomplished as a result of the FYRA (First Year Research Award) program. As soon as we began the research process in the fall semester, we were immersed in writing center literature, which helped us further develop our research question. Then, in the spring semester, we went through the semester-long training course to become advisors in the Writing Center. (A little bit backwards, we know!) We also participated in the Naylor Workshop on Undergraduate Research in Writing Studies and presented at both regional and international writing center conferences. How many people can say all that about their first two years in college?

Though all those opportunities and experiences have made our research experience unique, one of our greatest takeaways has been the unexpected but strong friendship this project has sparked. Amidst the hours of norming and the midnight number-crunching sessions and the seven-hour road trips (complete with karaoke!), our team grew pretty dang close. At this point, trying to explain our relationship to people has gotten rather complex. It usually goes something like this: "They're my friends, but they also work at the Writing Center with me, and they're my co-researchers for this really hard-to-explain research project we're doing." Neither our friendship nor our research project would be complete without the other. In this reflection, we hope to shed some light on the experiences of three undergraduate researchers and highlight the work we have done over the last two years studying asynchronous eTutoring comments.

Our research focuses on one of the challenges writing centers face: often, we have no tangible results from our sessions. There is no paper trail, no way to tell what kinds of changes writers make, if any. As writing center sessions center around tutor feedback, the inability of tutors to know if writers are finding their suggestions helpful prevents growth for both parties. To address this shortcoming, we elected to analyze papers submitted through eTutoring on our writing center software, WCONLINE. This route allows for a record of first drafts and tutors' comments, which appear on the right side of Microsoft Word documents. For those students who resubmit their papers, we can see the revisions that correspond to those comments. Our research taps into the potential of this record as we analyzed the overall effectiveness of asynchronous eTutoring comments. To analyze the asynchronous eTutoring comments, we mainly utilized Stephen Witte and Lester Faigley's 1981 taxonomy of revision changes from "Analyzing Revision."

Because we were all completely new to the writing center field at the beginning of our research process, a lot of these concepts felt particularly slippery. We spent our first semester solely reading articles about rhetoric, composition, and writing center theory and practice, but it still felt insufficient compared to the decades others had spent developing and refining these ideas. This is one of the characteristics that makes our experience as undergraduate researchers unique. So, it was (understandably) challenging for us to comprehend how our work fit into that larger picture. On that front, we're still learning; one of the biggest comments we got at the Naylor Workshop was to read a well-known scholar of asynchronous eTutoring whose work we had somehow missed in our review of the literature. Another difficulty was the taxonomy itself. Between the vagueness of the categories and the occasional ambiguity of the tutors' comments, we spent hours alone trying to categorize our comments, only to spend more hours defending our choices when we met for norming. Those hours of norming, however, became some of the first building blocks of our relationship, allowing us to strengthen not only our research but also our teamwork and friendship.

And, one of the most powerful moments for us as researchers came from our struggles with that taxonomy. For nearly a year by that point, we had been working with a revised version of the taxonomy, including two categories we had added, and thought little of it. We received feedback from one of the mentors at the Naylor Workshop recommending that we claim this taxonomy as a product of our own research, a moment which opened our eyes to our legitimacy and power as researchers. Through this experience, we learned how research is very much a living process; by metaphorically standing on the shoulders of others, we were able to see a bit farther into the growing field of writing center work. Though we are still basically newbies in the field, we are leaving our mark. (At least we hope to!) Going forward, we plan to write and submit an article soon and see it published before we graduate.

Since then, we've definitely encountered more confusion and roadblocks, but our team and project have flourished. Extending past the intended end date of the FYRA program, our work has continued through our second year at Wittenberg as well. This opportunity allowed us to travel to three conferences and workshops in a six-month period. Though our journey may be coming to an end, we will continue to be mentors for the upcoming Writing Center FYRA recipients. They may not have the same amazing whirlwind of experiences that we did—either professionally or socially—but we will pass on to them the lesson we learned from conducting research together: inexperience can foster innovation.

Works Cited

Faigley, Lester and Stephen Witte. "Analyzing Revision." *College Composition and Communication*, vol. 32, no. 4, 1981, pp. 400-414.

Multimedia Undergraduate Research in Composition

Hannah Bellwoar, Jill Palmer, and Fisher Stroud

Juniata College

At Juniata, a small liberal arts college, faculty and students have a lot of freedom in what forms their research can take. Jill and Fisher are seniors at Juniata, both working on multimedia research projects; Hannah is their faculty mentor and a faculty member in professional writing and integrated media arts. We believe that in the field of composition, faculty mentors should be encouraging students and providing research experiences with similar freedom so students can work in multimedia forms and address audiences that are relevant to them.

Hannah: Mentoring Creative, Multimedia Undergraduate Research

As a graduate student in the early 2000s, my faculty mentors Gail Hawisher and Paul Prior provided opportunities for creative, multimedia research in my writing studies classes. We read Joyce Walker's "Textural Textuality," a nonlinear piece of digital scholarship; we made our scholarship into multimedia forms such as websites, collages, cookies, and 3D objects; and we embodied the digital and cultural-historic activity theory scholarship with which we engaged. Making multimedia scholarship energized and engaged me; as I played with theory, I began to understand and feel it, as Jody Shipka puts it, developing rhetorical and material awareness. I've continued to write and publish multimedia and digitally-born scholarship since then.

    As I was finishing my degree in 2010, Cheryl Ball was making her tenure case, arguing for "scholarship that uses appropriate, multiple media—writing, audio, video, graphics, coding, etc.—to enact its argument and typically cannot be printed and retain its meaning." I thought to myself: why isn't the multimedia scholarship that I produce as highly valued as print scholarship, when it has such an important impact on me and the audiences I want to reach? When I got my job at Juniata and started mentoring undergraduate research in writing studies, it was never a question of whether I would provide my students opportunities to work in multiple media to develop rhetorical and material awareness and to impact and engage the audiences important to them.

    What I didn't realize was the tremendous reciprocity involved in mentoring undergraduate research. Through this work, I've continued to refine my teaching, encouraging students to do multimedia research in my classes and expand those projects into their senior research.

Jill: Combining Writing and Digital Media

When I began my college experience as a freshman, I assumed that my final project would be a paper of some kind. However, I became interested in multimedia because of different classes, such as Video Production Writing, Intro to Professional Writing, and Visual Literacy. These classes helped me realize the other ways that I could manifest my research to reflect the writing and digital media parts of my major. Because I studied both writing and digital media during my college career, I felt that the best way to display what I had learned over my time as a student was by creating text-based, interactive, fictional game. In my game, the player takes on the role of the first human engineer on board Starship Lunus, a largely Martian organization located somewhere in the Andromeda galaxy. The purpose of this game is to bring attention to workplace discrimination through a workforce simulation experience. This research project gave me the opportunity to explore nonlinear storytelling techniques through constructing a narrative with multiple endings. This melding of my dual passions makes my project unique because I force my audience to engage in multiple different ways. Part of my project involved presenting my research to a class of sophomore English students so that they could begin to imagine what their own final senior projects could be. By choosing a nontraditional senior thesis and sharing it with others, I am altering other students' perceptions of what a professional writing senior thesis could.

Fisher: Putting Research into a Representational Medium

I have spent most of my degree studying Marshall McLuhan's famous phrase: "The medium is the message." And I find my research experience differed from those of my peers, because I had to demonstrate what I had learned about media in a much more abstract way. When I began my degree, I wasn't aware that I was going to be able to create a multimedia project as undergraduate research; as soon as I saw that opportunity, however, I knew that it was the perfect choice for me. Being able to realize that research by creating a short film that examines the limits and constraints of the medium seems like the most appropriate way to culminate my degree.

The opportunity to do undergraduate research has been such an educational experience for me, and I also appreciate the opportunity to invite others to participate in that research. Being able to collaborate with my peers as cast and crew and giving them the opportunity to gain experience working on a student film is really valuable to me. I know how valuable that experience is because it's the same way that I learned about the opportunity to work on a multimedia project, through working on my peers' films over the past three years.

Conclusion

We believe that multimedia research doesn't have to be a difficult process, though it could seem difficult for mentors and undergraduate students at first—especially if it is something they are not as used to. Each of us incorporated our interests and took on new challenges with multimedia research. We recommend that undergraduate students take advantage of opportunities for multimedia research as early as possible in their undergraduate coursework. We urge students to talk to their professors about their interests and not to be discouraged at the possibility of doing multimedia research because it seems difficult. We had preconceived notions about what is allowed in academia, but we've learned that composition scholars do multimedia research and that some scholarly endeavors can more fully represent the research through multimedia means. We believe in the deep engagement provided when students are free to combine their interests with their coursework and pursue research in multiple media to reach the audiences that matter to them.

Works Cited

Ball, Cheryl E. "Research Statement." Received by Provost Everts, *Dr. Cheryl E. Ball*, 2009, ceball.com/research/tenure-letter/.

McLuhan, Marshall. *Understanding Media: Extensions of Man*. Signet, 1966.

Shipka, Jody. *Towards a Composition Made Whole*. U of Pittsburgh P, 2011.

Walker, Joyce. "Textural Textuality: A Personal Exploration of Critical Race Theory." *Kairos* 7.1, 2002. http://kairos.technorhetoric.net/7.1/binder.html?features/walker/text/index.html

Book Reviews

Social Media Ethics and the Rhetorical Tradition

Rhetoric, Technology, and the Virtues, by Jared S. Colton and Steve Holmes. Utah State UP, 2018. 184 pp.

Social Writing/Social Media: Publics, Presentations, and Pedagogies, edited by Douglas M. Walls and Stephanie Vie. WAC Clearinghouse/UP of Colorado, 2017. 348 pp.

Reviewed by Kristine L. Blair, Duquesne University

At the Obama Foundation Summit in October 2019, former President Barack Obama questioned the efficacy of social media users who rely on Twitter and other popular forums to foster a "call-out" or "woke culture" that he assessed was often more judgmental and intolerant than activist (Rueb and Taylor). As a public rhetorician, Obama was encouraging the young people attending the summit to consider the affordances of online public discourse in fostering ethical behavior and more genuine forms of activism. However insightful and newsworthy, Obama's assessment of much of today's public discourse is not a new argument. Indeed, it reflects the wisdom of the classical rhetoricians themselves, from the older sophist Protagoras's assertion that rhetoric could be used to make the worse case appear the better (Poster), to Aristotle's definition of rhetoric for the ages, "the faculty of observing in any given case the available means of persuasion" (*Rhetoric*).

Scholarship in digital rhetoric and composition is often theoretically and pedagogically focused on moving students and citizens from passive consumers of information to harnessing digital tools for their own personal and professional goals through civic action. We see this in both alphabetic and multimodal form via hashtag activism, from #MeToo and #BlackLivesMatter to #TakeaKnee, as well as visual rhetorical remixes across social media platforms. This includes not only hashtags but meme culture as well. Consider the case of Grumpy Cat, aka Tardar Sauce, the perennially frowning feline star of such popular memes as "I Don't like Mondays" and "I Like the Sound You Make When You Shut Up" (Menendez). Just as President Obama's commentary about call-out culture made international headlines, so too did Grumpy Cat's death earlier in 2019. As her Wikipedia page reports, Grumpy Cat had a combined social media network following of over twelve million viewers.

Be it a former president of the United States, a feline internet celebrity, the tweets of our current President that drive the daily news cycle, or the rise of internet influencers and vloggers marketing products and lifestyles, social media networks are multimodal and multigenred, multivocal and multilingual, and inherently rhetorical as they both persuade and entertain. Certainly, as Protagoras and Obama suggest, these online networks can make the worse case appear the better in ways that have led to questions about information ethics in an era of algorithmic rhetorical practices that attempt to influence the digital public and the digital electorate.

As a result of such diverse digital rhetorical artifacts that are produced, distributed, and consumed within and across equally diverse digital discourse communities, we are less focused on the question of *whether* to study today's social media networks as rhetorical composing but more attuned to applying an array of rhetorical and ethical frameworks, methods, and methodologies, within both academic and public contexts. Two recent, and I would argue necessary, books that ground the study of social media in the rhetorical tradition are Jared S. Colton and Steve Holmes's *Rhetoric, Technology, and the Virtues* and Douglas M. Walls's and Stephanie Vie's collection *Social Writing/Social Media: Publics, Presentations, and Pedagogies*. Both books suffer the fate of print discussions of social media; the dynamic Twitterverse alone populates and circulates at a velocity for which the static nature of print scholarship can never catch up in terms of applying rhetorical theory to contemporary practice, including the 2016 election and its aftermath. Nevertheless, the powerful scope of these rhetorical and ethical discussions provides useful models to replicate in even the most current social media life and news cycle.

Central to Colton and Holmes's argument is the emphasis on Aristotelian virtue ethics as a neglected paradigm "grounded in the dispositions individuals develop through their daily living practices—practices in the present that increasingly involve social media and digital technologies" (5). In my own work, I have relied heavily on Stuart Selber's triumvirate of functional, critical, and rhetorical literacies stemming from his 2004 *Multiliteracies for a Digital Age*. Yet, like many of my colleagues, I have always posited that the emphasis on ethics is an equally vital component, thus making Colton and Holmes's contribution to the scholarly conversation on digital rhetorics a compelling one. While the authors acknowledge that Aristotelian virtue ethics is not a singular framework to identify ethical affordances and challenges in digital rhetorical practices, they skillfully align this framework with contemporary theorists and philosophers that include Jacques Rancière, Adriana Cavarero, Martha Nussbaum, and Jane Bennett and situate their work in current digital rhetorical theory.

The book first articulates an operational definition of virtue ethics by juxtaposing Aristotelian concepts from *Nicomachean Ethics* with three specific frameworks: *utilitarianism*, the evaluation of behavior based on its greater good for a vast majority, with its roots in the philosophies of Jeremy Bentham and John Stuart Mill; *deontology*, the assessment of actions based on their adherence to existing ethical or moral principles, a la Immanuel Kant; and *postmodernism*, a more fluid attention to cultural and ideological as opposed to universal conditions that drive the definition and evaluation of ethical behavior in both digital and non-digital contexts, relying on philosophers from Jean-François Lyotard and Michel Foucault to rhetoricians such as James Berlin and James Porter. In many ways the postmodern most closely meshes with rhetoric, connected to the concept of *Kairos* and more sophistic and democratic conceptions of knowledge-making through language. What differentiates these and other postmodern approaches, according to the authors, is a frequent rejection of ethical frameworks based on utilitarian and deontological value systems. In contrast, a virtue ethics framework is dependent on Aristotle's and the authors' subsequent emphasis on *hexis*, or the habits and dispositions impacting "decision making across multiple and contingent rhetorical situations" (12) and the emergence of these habits, both good and bad, in social media contexts.

Consequently, Colton and Holmes organize their resulting discussion around a series of diverse technological genres and modalities to document how virtue ethics offers rhetoric and composition scholars a better understanding of the digital habits of everyday users. I would agree that given our current digital moment, such a process is necessary from both a critical literacy standpoint, in terms of helping students and future citizens decipher human and algorithmic rhetorical practices, and from a rhetorical literacy standpoint, in terms of helping those same students and citizens develop habits that positively contribute to the communities in which they participate. In this way, *Rhetoric, Technology, and the Virtues* questions what it means to be ethically literate in the digital age. Colton and Holmes prove the power of a virtue ethics framework in its application to several specific genres: closed captioning through video production, digital sampling and remix, and "slacktivism."

Given recent discussions of accessibility and the prominence of disability studies in rhetoric and composition and computers and writing, the emphasis on closed captioning is significant. Here, the authors deploy Jacques Rancière's theory of active equality as a "hexis of social justice" to challenge closed captioning as both an ethical and, in some contexts, unethical practice. Thus, the authors challenge mere captioning for captioning's sake, with more focus on how the use of such captioning is part of the meaning- and knowledge-making process of digital rhetorical composing. A related concern is the ideological nature of that process, particularly in those instances where captions are used to reinforce cultural stereotypes. For the authors, Rancière's emphasis on equality aligns with intentional, rhetorically effective practices that benefit users. Within a *hexis of social justice* captioning is considered a foundational aspect of the composing process rather than supplemental to it. Although Colton and Holmes provide several helpful strategies for how instructors could enact these goals in the classroom, some of these hypothetical examples could use more balance with actual pedagogical practices by the authors themselves or by teacher-scholars doing similar work in order to better acknowledge the limits and the admitted challenges of deploying such goals. Ultimately, both Rancière and Aristotle represent "a hexis that a digital rhetorician must constantly cultivate in order to practice active forms of social justice within workplace situations and research practices" (73).

The authors further advocate for a *hexis of care* in their next chapter on digital sampling. While discussions of remix and digital sampling have typically focused on copyright, intellectual property, and fair use (see, for example, Lawrence Lessig's *Remix: Making Art and Commerce Thrive in the Hybrid Economy* or Martine Rife's *Invention, Copyright, and Digital Writing*), Colton and Holmes apply Adriana Cavarero's philosophies of vocal expression and vulnerability to define a hexis of care as addressing "the kinds of questions we should be asking in our own digital rhetoric pedagogies and practices that draw on sampling—questions that interrogate how other cultures, traditions, and people are represented and acknowledged" (80). The chapter includes many useful examples, notably from popular music, to articulate, via Cavarero and from what seems a lesser extent in this case Aristotle, a heuristic of vulnerability to assess the motives and consequences for digital sampling practices, whether they are in fact caring or, conversely, wounding. These questions are exceptionally useful in both theoretical and pedagogical contexts, and the authors synthesize various perspectives on sampling, from appropriating at will regardless of cultural origins, to advocating a more visible, respectful acknowledgment of the cultures and communities represented in such remixes.

The final two hexeis involve issues of *generosity* and *patience*. In their chapter on social media technology, Colton and Holmes connect Aristotle's and Martha Nussbaum's respective takes on generosity, the latter reflecting the ability to give, without expecting a return on investment, to slacktivism. Here, a virtue ethics approach questions the dispositions that may evolve from such online activities in both virtual and face-to-face contexts. The primary example driving the chapter is the "Humans of New York" website and its growth into a space for online philanthropy and social justice, successful in "creating a set of conditions in which the disposition of generosity can be cultivated in what many of us would consider to be a stereotypical slacktivist space" (96). Such models, whether it be the Ice Bucket Challenge also featured in the chapter, or even as I write this essay, the current worldwide response to the bushfires in Australia, may inevitably challenge the binary between the online and offline and the ways in which today's hashtag activist culture has undoubtedly fostered a hexis of generosity even if it is less visible in physical settings, a clear affordance of social media in circulating information, values, and ethics.

In their chapter on the hexis of patience, Colton and Holmes turn to environmental activist rhetorics, including the process of shaming individuals online for their lack of environmental responsibility in what the authors identify as a form of epideictic rhetoric. Consistent with other chapters, virtue ethics are combined with contemporary philosophy, in this case, Jane Bennett's new materialist frameworks that extend the notion of agency to both human and non-human actants, something the authors accurately note is a current focus in rhetorical studies. In reacting against outrage and anger, both Aristotle and Bennett foreshadow the concerns that former president Barack Obama raises about "woke" and "call-out culture," thus making the discussion, even with fewer timely examples, a highly relevant one for today's digital age. Colton and Holmes conclude the book by advocating for a hexis based in part on Bruno Latour's "virtue of fairness," which not only disrupts the binary between human and machine but examines "how networks and actors support behaviors as opposed to previously settled topoi alone" (143). This point reinforces Aristotelian virtue ethics and complementary rhetorics and philosophies as dynamic and responsive to the online spaces that shape them, undoubtedly a viable analytical framework.

Because I identify prominently as a Computers and Writing specialist and have participated in that discourse community for several decades, I can't help but sense an occasional disjointedness between theory and application in the text. Some additional inclusion of work that more specifically addresses issues of accessibility, digital activism/slacktivism would help to create a more recursive relationship between theory and practice as well as broaden the audience scope for this important discussion, notably because Colton and Holmes identify their audiences to be both novice and expert, and both researcher and practitioner. They denote their intended audience as "digital rhetoricians," which is appropriate given their topic and their reliance on Doug Eyman's definition of digital rhetoric as "the application of rhetorical theory (as an analytic method or heuristic for production) to digital texts and performances" (qtd. 6). Yet the sub-discipline of Computers and Writing seems oddly peripheral; despite some citations from this area, it is seemingly absent from the authors' early delineation of the field in their introduction. Because the book's purpose is also to orient newcomers, this is a minor concern in what is a solidly recursive relationship between social media practices and both rhetorical and ethical traditions.

For this reason, another recent book, *Social Writing/Social Media: Publics, Presentations, and Pedagogies*, is a notable complement in extending academic and popular contexts where ethical and rhetorical composing can and do flourish. Both books stress the rhetoricity of social media, and in their introduction, Douglas M. Walls and Stephanie Vie remind us of how Barack Obama had been dubbed the first "social media President," something that the era of Donald Trump as the current tweeter-in-chief makes clear the ubiquitous and forever present role these tools play in our personal, public, and civic lives. Through their skillful assemblage of sixteen chapters across three sections, "Publics and Audiences"; "Presentations of Self, Groups, and Data"; and "Pedagogy," the editors and contributors confirm that social media rhetorics flourish within writing classrooms and our resulting digital writing research methods and methodologies. Again, these are not new areas, but as Heidi A. McKee and Dánielle Nicole DeVoss's 2007 collection, *Digital Writing Research: Technologies, Methodologies, and Ethical Issues,* questioned, "How are computerized technologies, particularly global technologies, raising new . . . ethical issues related to privacy, individual rights, and representation? . . . Given the continually evolving state of technology and human interactions with and through technological affordances, what preparation do future researchers need?" (4). Despite the decade's difference between these two collections' publication, these questions remain central and, in the case of Walls and Vie's compilation, are addressed by a current group of social media writing researchers working in even more diverse academic, public, and communal contexts than perhaps we may have imagined over a decade ago, when Facebook, Twitter, and YouTube were in their respective infancy and toddler stages, and Instagram was not yet conceived.

Part One, "Publics and Audiences," provides a broad swath of social media's impact on activism, critical literacies, and community building, and the ways various rhetorical exigencies build and sustain virtual forums. In ways that align with Colton and Holmes, there is implicit attention in a number of chapters to the ethical dimensions. For example, Caroline Dadas's lead chapter "Hashtag Activism: The Promise and Risk of 'Attention'," offers users strategies for engaging in such digital advocacy that not only deploy the affordances of Twitter and other platforms but also help activists understand cultural, historical, and political contexts, the role of "rhetorical velocity" and circulation, and the need to align their work with reputable coverage of the issues at hand. Dadas's case study includes #bringbackourgirls and #yesallwomen to document the ways hashtags can be decontextualized, repurposed, and remixed for differing ideological purposes and thus encourages further attention to the consequences of these and other activist campaigns. Chapters such as Estee Beck's encourage us to consider the ethics of online sharing and prosumerism in an age of algorithmic surveillance and promotes "learning how to identify, analyze, and possibly subvert structures of power and enable critical consciousness" (50) in both classroom and community spaces. Although there is an explicit and not inaccurate assumption throughout the book that social media participation is endemic to our culture, Cory Bullinger and Stephanie Vie's "After a Decade of Social Media: Abstainers and Ex-Users" provides an important counterpoint, advocating research on those who have opted out and questioning how such non-users are defined by others or depicted in the larger culture, how they define themselves, and how they articulate their motivations for not engaging online. Whether it be due to privacy and safety concerns (something of great import given Beck's earlier chapter), time constraints in light of managing an online presence, or simply as a form of dissent from the ubiquity of digital platforms, non-users are as vital a population to foreground in social media research as their connected counterparts.

Part Two, "Presentation of Self, Groups, and Data," relies on a range of mixed-methods studies to interrogate the participation and identity choices users make, including students. Bronwyn T. Williams's chapter on polymedia device usage among students reflects decisions about how they choose to maintain relationships and the role of emotion in those choices. Whether it's a student maintaining telephone contact with a parent because of the parent's comfort-level with the medium, or participating in forums because of a sense of belonging with other friends in that particular space, Williams rightly concludes that given "the role of mobile digital technologies in creating and nurturing relations, we should see it not as replacement, nor an add-on, but as an integral part of daily life" (141). Personal and community interaction is also critical to Amber Buck's "Grad School 2.0: Performing Professionalism on Social Media," as she details her case study of three graduate students and their ten-month social networking activities, including connecting with scholars in areas of interest and expertise, live tweeting conferences, and representing personal and professional identities in online forums. Buck's chapter has important implications for mentoring graduate students at a crucial point in their professional careers as their continued navigation of expectations—both online and off—impact the role of social media in that identify formation. Other chapters in the section foreground the important role of cultural rhetorics and identities to promote accessibility, empowerment, and social justice. As Les Hutchinson concludes in her chapter relating to anonymity, "Not every Twitter user has the same privilege to participate in online conversations freely without consequences. Most of us to have to account for our social positions, genders, politics, even our sexualities when we speak online" (201). Hutchinson profiles her own efforts to subvert and reject traditional performances of gender to develop a queered feminist identity and the possibilities and constraints of anonymity in that process. But even access to supportive forums does not guarantee activism, engagement, and empowerment. This is something Kristin L. Arola has observed firsthand, as she reports in her chapter, "Indigenous

Interfaces," contending that such networks can exist and be deployed even in concert with other facets of our identities, even in forums like Facebook.

Space constraints do not allow me to include every chapter in my overview of this collection's many strengths, including the final section, "Pedagogy." Lilian W. Mina's "Social Media in the Writing Class: The New Digital Divide" reports the results of a survey of instructors to determine their use of social media in the writing classroom, with the dominant rationale including helping students understand rhetorical choices, analyzing online content, developing critical and reflective thinking, and improving overall writing skills. Similarly, Michael J. Faris's chapter, "Contextualizing Students' Media Ideologies and Practices," collects diverse data to focus in this case on student perceptions of their use of these tools in the classroom, including how they interacted with teachers and with each other. Faris provides a useful heuristic to help teachers ground their social media pedagogies in institutional contexts and ideologies in ways that benefit students. Finally, Chris M. Anson's concluding chapter to the collection, "Intellectual, Argumentative, and Informational Affordances of Public Forums: Potential Contributions to Academic Learning," reminds us of the collection's goals, our responsibility to bridge the gap between academic and self-sponsored literacies, and our commitment to continued research that strengthens our own and our students' knowledge about the rhetorical affordances of digital and multimodal texts and contexts.

I am completing this review essay while watching an episode of MSNBC's *MTP Daily*, where anchor Chuck Todd's feature "I'm Obsessed With" focuses on the hashtag #bigiftrue, noting that although Twitter users are not expected to be fact checkers, citizens should take responsibility for their retweets. After a series of parody #bigiftrue examples, Todd states that "If you think #bigiftrue absolves you of social media sin, well that's wrong. Before you Tweet, think." In an era of fake news, social bots, and algorithmic rhetorics that influence our consumer habits and our decision making, including Cambridge Analytica's psychographical and inherently unethical practices that so influenced the 2016 Presidential election, the question of social media's rhetorical affordances is a compelling one.

One lingering concern, despite the useful discussions of access and social justice that aligns both books, is a lesser emphasis on more global networks. For example, while it has been important to see the impact of Tarana Burke's original activism and creation of the Me Too movement on behalf of sexual assault survivors that is now part of the #MeToo hashtag origin story (when initially it wasn't), not everyone has access to the tools and the freedoms to engage in such online solidarity. The #MeToo movement has looked different in China, for example, where instead of overt references to #MeToo, the emojis and words for "rice" and "bunny" replace the powerful hashtag (Anderson), given that the words for "rice bunny" in Chinese are "mi too," a subversive way to express solidarity and resist censorship.

Overall, the authors and editors of these two books have provided analytical frameworks, mixed-method research studies, and powerful calls to action for their audiences to take social media seriously, lest we do find the worse case to be made the better. As Chuck Todd aptly concludes his segment, if we heed these calls, "Twitter would be a better, happier place. And if that were true, that would be big." This call applies to all online rhetorical spaces, and the power of both *Rhetoric, Technology, and the Virtues* and *Social Writing/Social Media: Publics, Presentations, and Pedagogies* is that these nascent 21st-century communication spaces are not supplemental to the classical rhetorical traditions of Protagoras, Aristotle, their respective contemporaries, and those who came after them. They are, in fact, a vital continuation and representation of rhetoric and writing as inherently powerful in impacting local and global audiences, and the resulting need to consider the ethical demands and consequences of that power.

Pittsburgh, Pennsylvania

Works Cited

Anderson, Margaret. "How Feminists in China Are Using Emoji to Avoid Censorship." *Wired*, 30 March 2018, https://www.wired.com/story/china-feminism-emoji-censorship. Accessed 9 Jan. 2020.

Aristotle. *Rhetoric*, translated by W. Rhys Roberts. The Internet Classics Archive, http://classics.mit.edu/Aristotle/rhetoric.1.i.html. Accessed 2 Jan. 2020.

McKee, Heidi A., and Dánielle Nicole DeVoss. *Digital Writing Research: Technologies, Methodologies and Ethical Issues*. Hampton Press, 2007.

Menendez, Elisa. "The 30 Most Iconic Grumpy Cat Memes." *Metro UK*, 17 May 2019, https://metro.co.uk/2019/05/17/30-iconic-grumpy-cat-memes-9586691/?ito=cbshare. Accessed 2 Jan. 2020.

MTP Daily with Chuck Todd. *MSNBC*. NBC Universal. 9 Jan. 2020.

Poster, Carol. "Protagoras." *Internet Encyclopedia of Philosophy*, https://www.iep.utm.edu/protagor. Accessed 2 Jan. 2020.

Rueb, Emily S., and Derek Bryson Taylor. "Obama on Call-Out Culture: 'That's Not Activism'." *New York Times*, 31 Oct. 2019, https://www.nytimes.com/2019/10/31/us/politics/obama-woke-cancel-culture.html. Accessed 2 Jan. 2020.

Selber, Stuart. *Multiliteracies for a Digital Age*. Southern Illinois UP, 2004.

Wikipedia Contributors. "Grumpy Cat." Wikipedia, Wikimedia Foundation, 18 Jan. 2020, en.wikipedia.org/wiki/Grumpy_Cat. Accessed 19 Jan. 2020.

Re/Orienting Writing Studies: Queer Methods, Queer Projects, edited by William P. Banks, Matthew B. Cox, and Caroline Dadas. Logan: Utah State UP, 2019. 240 pp.

Reviewed by Katrina L. Miller, University of Nevada, Reno

We all know what methodology does: it provides a path forward through uncertain intellectual terrain, guides our curiosities in generative ways, grants legitimacy to our idiosyncratic interests within academic spaces, and allows others to follow in our footsteps. As members of a discipline born from an often-uncomfortable marriage of humanities and social science, we also know that methodology can constrict, limit, colonize, co-opt, and oppress.

In *Re/Orienting Writing Studies*, the authors argue that queer methods and methodologies can help us acknowledge how "research methodologies work to reproduce the same knowledge in the same frameworks we're already comfortable exploring" (192). This book serves as a welcomed reminder of the potential of research, that raw and messy knowledge-making process that requires some degree of risk.

To be honest, reviewing this book made me nervous; I wasn't sure if it was for me. The review copy landed on my desk the same month I stepped off the tenure-track. I'd chosen to take a teaching-focused position in a locale that better suited my wife's career and the needs of our family, including our young children and aging parents. I was not in the headspace of thinking about research and felt relief at the prospect of re-focusing my career on undergraduate teaching and writing program administration. My now-much- shorter list of potential and in-progress research projects did not include anything I'd label as a "queer project." Yet, as Pamela Takayoshi writes in the preface of this collection, "All writing researchers work in heteronormative cultures and navigate normative binaries . . . [and] . . . this book shows us how to be aware of those (often invisible) normative forces and how to navigate them in the conduct of ethical research" (xiii). Queer research methods and methodologies are something we all can (and the authors in this collection would argue *should*) tap into in order to reframe our work in ways that helps us question and critique what is normative and hegemonic and follow through on our theoretical, epistemological, and *ethical* commitments.

Much like other collections recently reviewed in the pages of this journal (e.g., Jacob Babb's review of *Composition, Rhetoric, and Disciplinarity*), this book attends to questions about the power and potential of disciplinarity, especially as it manifests and reifies through research. This collection adds valuable perspectives, united by a common thread of examining and inhabiting research as way to resist heteronormativity. Across eleven chapters, the contributors (all emerging and early career researchers) explore the possibilities of queer methodologies and methods. Taken together, this collection posits (and deconstructs) answers to those disciplinary questions that are new and compellingly different. Spoiler alert: there's also a surprising number of f-bombs.

In the introductory chapter, Banks, Cox, and Dadas explain how this collection addresses a significant elision in the field: the scarcity of methodology scholarship relevant to queer researchers and/or queer subjects. Even after decades of landmark work on queer rhetoric and queer composition (they cite commonly referenced work in queer theory, such as Alexander and Wallace, 2009; Malinowitz 1995; Alexander, 2008; Rhodes, 2004; Rallin, 2008; Halberstam, 2011), queer work remains marginalized and poorly understood. They boldly note that writing studies has disregarded or dismissed the queer turn in the field, as identified by Alexander and Wallace (2009). For example, they refer to the 2013 WPA Conference theme: Queering the Writing Program. Outside of the plenary sessions focused on queer-work, most presenters ignored the theme and consequently declined the invitation to engage with queer inquiry work (6). Part of the issue, they note, is an "inclusionary mindset" that adds sexual minorities to "our menu of identitarian concerns" (7). It is difficult to move beyond this misconception, but the introductory chapter defines queer rhetorics and queer methodologies in a way that should resonate with teacher-researchers with a variety of backgrounds and interests. For example, they discuss *discourse* and *performativity* as two familiar concepts in writing studies that were foundational to early queer scholarship.

At once concerned with knowledge creation about topics we might think of as queer and the relationships among researchers who identify as queer, this collection provides an array of perspectives on queer inquiry. These perspectives, the editors argue, are a necessary antidote to the discipline's "conservative" tendencies that may have led to the omission of queer inquiry methodology. Rather than prescribe a limited number of approaches, this collection focuses on relational and interpretive elements of queer theory. And, unlike other collections, this book is not divided into thematic or chronological sections. Even though the editors purposefully resist cohesion, my review of the chapters focuses on themes or commonalities between the chapters.

Hillery Glasby and Deborah Kuzawa offer the most pedagogically focused chapters. Glasby advocates for two queer concepts—ambivalence and failure—which she explored in her junior-level composition course focused on LGBTQ identities and writing. She describes the design of the course, reading list, and, importantly, the final multimodal project for the course that asked students to describe and analyze how they have "erased, silenced, and written" as well as how they "(re)present and (re)write" themselves (33). Her reflection on this assignment explains the ways that students took risks, played, and violated expectations as they wrote about moments of uncertainly and struggle, reflecting more insightful and complex thinking as they abandoned conventional expectations for academic writing. Likewise, Kuzawa shares her method of using queer theory with her first-year writing students as they explored the Digital Archive of Literacy Narratives (DALN). She argues that the DALN can be used in writing classrooms to demonstrate and practice queer inquiry by providing artifacts that can be interpreted using queer methods and analytical structures.

Others eschew pedagogical concerns to focus on queer research methodologies—especially blended methodologies—that could be adopted and adapted by other researchers. For example, Chanon Adsanatham promotes a "methodological alliance" between queer theory and comparative rhetoric as both perspectives "value excess, absences, and multiplicities… in order to drive epistemological and social change" (79). He proposes a heuristic for conducting cross-cultural rhetorical readings of nonnormative rhetorical artifacts that includes five components: recontemplation, defamiliarization, reevaluation, ethics of care, and seeking incongruities (79). This heuristic, which he refers to as REDRES, is the most neatly packaged and portable method in the collection because it demonstrates how queer methods can be used as something more than a corrective for calls for increased "diversity" and can highlight epistemic and ethical consequences of cross-cultural rhetorics.

Maria Novotny similarly identifies queer theory as a "methodological ally" to narrative theory in her chapter on infertility stories as counterstories (113). Engaging the growing field of biomedical rhetorics, Novotny uses a queer assemblage method to attend to gaps in common infertility narratives by highlighting embodied non-normativities. A counterstory, she argues, disrupts dominant cultural narratives about in/fertility, facilitates more nuanced examinations of "spaces of becoming," and illuminates presumptions about who is impacted by infertility (122).

Moving away from qualitative methods, G Patterson explores how to queer quantitative research "challenge[s] the violence of objectivity that so often inspires suspicion of quantitative methods" raised by queer and trans theorists (56). Patterson explains how they adapted their initially qualitative survey to include mostly closed-ended questions designed to provide numerical data and, importantly, *why* these changes were needed and what new insights arose from queering survey design. Patterson also describes a "queer/trans kinship" method for recruiting survey participants. The chapter is an example of how any research method can be adjusted to promote more fairness and justice and provides a compelling case for reconceptualizing "deviations as untapped, rich sources of information rather than a methodological problem" (69).

Jean Bessette promotes queer historiography of rhetoric, literacy, and pedagogy as a means of strategically utilizing the past for contemporary ends concerned with fairness and justice. With a focus on the Lesbian Herstory Archives, Bessette explores binary pairs that often constrain the work of queer historiography—queer/archive, silence/speech, gossip/truth, fiction/history, present/past, and identity/alterity—and argues that queer historiography attuned to these conceptually complex binaries can help us uncover and generate "new understandings of what queer rhetoric, pedagogy, and worldmaking is and does—and hasn't done" (109).

The last two chapters explore methods for queering our work at the programmatic level. Nicole Caswell and Stephanie West-Puckett leverage Sara Ahmed's work on feminist killjoys to queer writing assessment and program assessment as "assessment killjoys" who disrupt and complicate the status quo notions of success and achievement within assessment work. Building on the social justice turn in writing assessment and critical theories of validity, Caswell and West-Puckett promote Queer Validity Inquiry, which they describe as "ongoing interrogation into the effects of assessment instruments…[that] intentionally refuses linear notions of progress and success" (170).

Dadas and Cox write about queer theory's potential in professional writing, noting the troubling disjuncture between professional writing's focus on the contextuality of effective writing and its reluctance to take up queer methods. They provide data from their survey of recent professional writing scholarship and an interview with Michelle Eble, who was then President of the Association of Teachers of Technical Writing. Their chapter concludes with concrete suggestions and heuristics for including queer methodologies and methods in professional writing research and a call for more research to debunk assumptions that professional writing is a space for normative rather than queer rhetorics.

Stacey Waite and Michael J. Faris offer the two most provocative chapters. Waite boldly (and playfully) presents an "instruction manual" for writing queer (42). Equal parts disorienting and inspiring, Waite's chapter deconstructs conventional advice for academic writing and instead offers disjointed, idiosyncratic advice. Her point is that such a manual is impossible. Faris's chapter presents a sensory autoethnography of his experiences on Grindr, a popular free social networking app that uses geolocation technology to connect users within a certain geographic range. These connections can be friendly or romantic but often lead to casual sexual encounters. These encounters, Faris argues, are a form of "impersonal intimacy" and impersonal rhetorical action (140). Faris positions his chapter as an interesting counterpoint to rhetoric's identitarian impulses and analyzes the materiality of sexual bodies as a corrective for queer inquiry work that focuses on sexuality as an identity rather than an action.

Conceptually indebted to traditions in feminist rhetorics and queer rhetorics, this collection expertly balances the instinct to contextualize cutting edge work within recognizable scholarly traditions, such as feminist rhetorics and queer theory, alongside the impulse to do something refreshingly different. The book would serve as a well-grounded introduction for teacher-researchers interested in queer inquiry work. As the editors rightly note, in the context of research methods courses for graduate students, this book would be best situated as a supplement to other collections on research methods and methodologies because it provides a provocative but theoretically grounded counterbalance to the more conservative and hegemonic tendencies within methodology scholarship. Emerging and early career scholars would likely see their own struggles with/against methodologies reflected in the pages of this collection, offering both validation of the struggle to marry research ideas and exigencies with recognized methods and providing potential ways through that struggle.

Reno, Nevada

Works Cited

Alexander, Jonathan. *Literacy, Sexuality, Pedagogy: Theory and Practice for Composition Studies*. Utah State UP, 2008.

Alexander, Jonathan, and David Wallace. "The Queer Turn in Composition Studies." *CCC*, vol. 61, no. 1, 2009, pp. W300-20.

Babb, Jacob. Review of *Composition, Rhetoric, and Disciplinarity* edited by Rita Malenczyk, Susan Miller-Cochran, Elizabeth Wardle, and Kathleen Blake Yancey. *Composition Studies*, vol. 47, no. 1, 2019, pp. 202-4.

Halberstam, Jack. *The Queer Art of Failure*. Duke UP, 2011.

Malinowitz, Harriet. *Textual Orientations: Lesbian and Gay Students and the Making of Discourse Communities*. Portsmouth: NH: Heinemann-Boyton/Cook, 1995.

Rallin, Aneil. "A Provocation: Queer is Not a Substitute for Gay/Lesbian." *Harlot: A Revealing Look at the Arts of Persuasion*, vol. 1, no. 1, 2008, harlotofthearts.org/index.php/harlot/article/view/5/3.

Rhodes, Jacqueline Jones. "Homo Origo: The Queertext Manifesto." *Computers and Composition*, vol. 21, no. 3, 2004, pp. 385-88, doi.org/10.1016/j.compcom.2004.05.001.

Serendipity in Rhetoric, Writing, and Literacy Research, edited by Maureen Daly Goggin and Peter N. Goggin. Logan: Utah State UP, 2018. 300 pp.

Reviewed by Michael Pak, University of Hawaiʻi – West Oʻahu

In first-year writing courses, I am often asked whether or not using first person pronouns are allowed. Behind this question are usually years of strict writing rules that forbid using "I" in academic writing. Instead of providing a simple answer to the question, I respond that it depends on the rhetorical situation. If there is an important reason to include yourself in the discourse—e.g., oral histories and personal essays—then using "I" makes perfect sense. Although Maureen Daly Goggin and Peter N. Goggin's edited anthology *Serendipity in Rhetoric, Writing, and Literacy Research* is a collection centered on the concept of serendipity in research, its main take-away is how integral the personal is in the writing process. Offering a variety of essays that examine how chance encounters and the unpredictable affect our academic research and writing, Goggin and Goggin's collection "restores the human element of storytelling about adventures in the making, unmaking, and dissemination of knowledge" (7). The collection forwards serendipity "as an unexpected rupture, and opportunity, fortunate circumstances, and discoveries," and each of the essays within explores how personal the performances of research can be (4).

Serendipity's first section, Intersections of Personal and Political, delves into the ways the process of research is often interwoven into our own lives. In Shirley E. Faulkner-Springfield's "'Oh, My God! He Was a Slave!' Secrets of a Virginia Courthouse Archive," the author shares how her archival research revealed that her great-great-grandfather had been "a resilient survivor of . . . [the] narrative of slavery" (26). By sharing her experience of research, Faulkner-Springfield's essay offers a "reinscribed," not revisionist, account of life writing and the history of race in America (26). Doreen Piano's "Making Sense of Disaster: Composing a Methodology of Place-Based Visual Research" locates herself in the midst of the disaster of Hurricane Katrina. Having moved to New Orleans three weeks before the storm, Piano's serendipitous timing "allowed [her] to rethink [her] connection to place and to others, often strangers, who had similar experiences" (39). Just as the rhetorical concept of *kairos* refers to opportunity of both time and place, Piano "make[s] the case for place as significant to the *where* and not just the *when* of serendipity" (29). Finally, in Gale Coskan-Johnson's "Death, Dying, and Serendipity," the author shares a constellation of personal and global events, such as 9/11 and the killing of

Osama bin Laden, to show how "disruption, frustration, and new connections" often serendipitously reveal new research trajectories (54).

Section two continues a focus on the personal in research and reminds us to keep our minds open and flexible. Lynèe Lewis Gaillet's essay argues that we need to prepare ourselves for serendipitous moments "by faithfully following our own interests and curiosity, working together, and keeping an open mind" (68). Caren Wakerman Converse shares an experience of revisiting personal experiences later with academic rigor and grounding; drawing from her experience as a former probation officer in her rhetorical analyses of pre-sentence investigation reports, Converse's narrative suggests the value of personal experience as a source of knowledge in the research process. Liz Rohan's "Echoes in the Archives" documents a journey researching the Northwestern University Settlement, where a chance detour to the Harriet Vittum Park revealed the limitations of archival work. Rohan's attention to the agency of archives, especially as it constructs the lives and legacies of women, reminds us of the tenuous existence of underrepresented people in history; "individual legacies can simply be lost to history because of scant records," and, unfortunately, sometimes luck and happenstance is needed for these narratives to reemerge (90). Kim Donehower wraps up the section with "Serendipity and Memory: The Value of Participant Observation," arguing that "vivid sensory impressions . . . melded with the emotions involved in participation may help certain memories more firmly take root" (98). As the *Serendipity* editors assert in their introduction, "chance favors only the prepared mind," and the four scholars in section two show us that a prepared mind is flexible, personal, traveled, and passionate (4).

The third section of the anthology, Stumbling into the Unknown, offers four narratives that explore how reality can be stranger than fiction, at least in the research process. From Maureen Daly Goggin's what-ifs that shine in her remembering of "her field research in churchyards, post offices, pubs, and museums in the English countryside" to Ryan Skinnell's serendipitous dissertation research process and Daniel Wuebben's searching for a missing Nikola Tesla street sign, the authors in section three share their personal essays to provide insight and commentary on the research (10). Peter N. Goggin's "The Art of the 'Accident': Serendipity in Field Research" reminds us that "serendipity is generally not one momentous happenstance but an accumulation of discoveries and events that emerge from purposeful exploration" (130). As random as research opportunities may seem, they are usually the culmination of a lot of disparate work, and Goggin does an excellent job of reminding readers not to get too carried away with the wonder that serendipity can seem to evoke; much of serendipity's existence relies on the work we have already done.

Having established the beneficial nature of being flexible and having an open mind to chance encounters in the research process, the collection moves on in section four to insist that researchers anticipate serendipity in their studies and discovery. In "Prepare to Be Surprised," Lori Ostergaard suggests having a flexible research agenda, a methodical approach that exhausts internet searches and library databases, and an organized approach to keep archival materials in their own catalogued contexts. Patty Wilde's "Playing the Name Game" reminds us that small differences in searches can yield quite different results. For example, while researching Loreta Janeta Velazquez, a Cuban-born woman who posed as a male Confederate soldier, Wilde discovered Velazquez's alias, Harry T. Buford; different spellings of her name like Madame L. J. Velasquez; and married names such as L. J. Velasquez Beard. Lynn Z. Bloom's "The Sunshine of Serendipity" shares her development of a canon of first-year writing essays, ranked by how many times individual authors were reprinted in readers spanning fifty years (from 1946-96). Bloom also shares a personal story of a student's serendipitous writing process of an honors project. In all, the essays in this fourth section exemplify how to use and account for serendipity in research and teaching.

Trusting the Process, the last section in the anthology, points out that serendipity does not always provide a nice eureka moment. Bill Endres, in "The Ethics of Serendipity," notes that serendipitous moments can sometimes arise from calamity or trauma, and that scholars need to consider ethical ramifications, especially for opportunities that are rare or fleeting (222). Brad Gyori argues that the unstable and unsettled aspects of postmodern rhetorical constructions—like remix, reboot, and deconstruction—are what become "legitimate process[es] of discovery" (245). Instead of having researchers focus "primarily on evidence that supports their argument du jour," disjunctive strategies like remixing and rebooting allow for chance and serendipity "to complicate and even confound the intuitions undergirding their proposed agendas" (244-5). Finally, for Zachary Beare, mischance can be just as productive as chance. In "The Strange Practices of Serendipitous Failure," Beare reinterprets the rhetorical concept of *metanoia* as missed opportunities, arguing that such a binary of *kairos*, or opportunity, deserves its own rhetorical consideration.

Although the collection's intentions are situated in research, readers who teach might be interested in more consideration of how to implement serendipity, conceptually or practically, into composition praxis. Some essays, like Bloom's, addresses serendipity in classroom narratives, but students can benefit from understanding how chance encounters and opportunities may shape their own research and writing. For instance, before embarking on research papers, I assign annotated bibliographies in first-year writing classes; however, instead of asking students to develop a strong research question upfront, I encourage them to jump directly into their research. I want students to understand that it is okay not to know exactly where research will take them. While *Serendipity*'s authors clearly agree with me in principle, I would have liked to see more examples of implementing concepts of *kairos*, as well as *metanoia*, for the writing classroom.

Yet, *Serendipity* is still a worthwhile read for teachers and researchers alike, particularly because of the theme of love—the love of learning and research, the love for our communities and personal histories—that threads through the many stories the contributors share with readers. Love is universal, and yet love is also personal, a duality of which the writers and editors continue to remind us. *Serendipity* reminds us that despite the tumultuous times in which we currently live and the "emboldened volatile discourses of intolerance and hatred" that feel rampant, compassion and open-mindedness, whether in research or in life, can keep us all positively invested in the worlds in which we live (12).

Kapolei, Hawaii

Black Perspectives in Writing Program Administration: From the Margins to the Center, edited by Staci M. Perryman-Clark and Colin Lamont Craig. Urbana: National Council for Teachers of English, 2019. 167 pp.

Reviewed by Floyd Pouncil, Michigan State University

As readers of this journal know, those who run writing programs—Writing Program Administrators, or WPAs—are typically university staff or faculty whose role is to organize the various aspects of writing that take place in formal academic learning settings, such as writing centers or the composition classroom. And, as with anything in the academy, the situation of WPAs in a post-secondary institution is one fraught with difficulties that are tied to present day social realities, like racism. *Black Perspectives in Writing Program Administration: From the Margins to the Center* presents to us the aforementioned situation in higher education, where WPAs are tasked with crafting curricula for students across institutions, in individual departments, and inside classrooms or writing centers that impact Black students and students of color who inhabit them. This impact, unfortunately, is often racist due to an uncritical engagement with the socio-historical context of race relations in the United States. Accordingly, editors Staci M. Perryman-Clark and Collin Lamont Craig—building on their previous work in writing program administration—seek to push against the racist orientation of writing programs and the WPAs who run them. Explicitly, they chose to focus this book deliberately and justly on Black students, Black faculty, Black WPAs, and Black experiences in the academy. They front these various sites as valuable to all who work in and alongside the classroom. Overall, *Black Perspectives* serves as a call-in to WPAs who want to do their work well within historical and present contexts of higher education.

In contrast to the historical realities of marginalization in higher education, Perryman-Clark and Craig forward a platform for self-reflection, reorientation, and action that centers Black students as a priority. This platform, then, provides a foundation for the collection's contributors: WPAs of color who do anti-racist work and speak to their lived experiences, White WPAs contending with their own position and research when it comes to anti-racist WPA work, teachers reflecting on developing and centering curricula on Black students through Afrocentric teaching methodologies, and other scholars expressing their interests in forwarding ways to explicitly implement anti-racist writing programs at historically Black colleges and universities (HBCUs) and predominantly White institutions (PWIs). The editors have gathered a specific set of practitioners who all orient themselves progressively towards working with anti-racist frameworks to counter what Asao Inoue, in the afterword, calls ". . . a White racial habitus in our judgement practices" (149).

Perryman-Clark and Craig chose each author in this short collection to shape the narrative that they are weaving about writing program administration. Grounding the overarching problem in local contexts, the introduction gives background on this project and takes readers through some of the racism the editors have encountered as WPAs. Chapters two and three focus on how two Black WPAs think through their positions and call for frameworks situated in Black ways of knowing. Specifically, in chapter two Carmen Kynard uses Afro-pessimism to discuss her refusal to orient herself in ways that allow White audiences to feel better about themselves and their work. She connects this to David F. Green Jr's use of the cypher in chapter three, where he argues, "Cyphers, at their best, provide pathways for contemplating how publics read and remember together, as well as how such interpretive work helps to address difference as a social, cultural, and material reality of all writing instruction" (52). In chapter three, Green builds upon Kynard's framework of survival as a Black WPA. He explains how current frameworks that many White practitioners take up are insufficient to the task of anti-racist WPA work.

Up to this point, the contributors have all been Black WPAs, but that changes when Scott Wible discusses his research on WPAs and his own position as a White male WPA doing anti-racist work in chapter four. Wible begins by discussing how his White contemporaries have not utilized opportunities to support and advocate for people of color; the root cause, as he identifies it, stems from his White colleagues who have not had to engage critically with White power dynamics in a way that would undermine their own positions of power in the academy. Even White WPAs like himself, who support anti-racist work, must push back against feelings of doing enough considering that " . . . without a radical break from the very ideological origins of black subjugation, such easily made solutions will, at best, only cater to the interests of white comfort and white fragility" (96). This chapter is important for White WPAs reading this collection as it builds upon Kynard's beliefs about decentering White WPAs' feelings; Wible models how feelings of adequacy are, in fact, admitting inadequacy. Chapters five and six take a different tone as the collection moves into practice. In contrast to the experiences discussed in chapters one through four, several contributors forward successful writing program models. The examples in these last two chapters can be thought of as useful heuristics for anti-racist and Afrocentric practitioners and WPA work broadly.

Specifically, chapter five is a moment where the collection breaks down how practitioners are doing the work of centering Black students in administration. Perryman-Clark and Craig begin by bringing our attention to an Afrocentric curriculum that demonstrates how we can focus on Black students' needs in the classroom. They invoke a definition of Afrocentric education from Molefi Kete Asante: " . . . a frame of reference wherein phenomena are viewed from the perspective of the African person. The Afrocentric approach seeks in every situation the appropriate centrality of the African person" (107). They also problematize some of the tried-and-true resources WPAs may utilize to build their curriculum, including the Council of Writing Program Administrators' online Assessment Gallery, which lacks insights from any HBCUs; the 2008 WPA Task Force on Internationalization, which has no mention of Sub-Saharan Africa; and the Framework for Success in Postsecondary Writing from the National Council of Teachers of English and the National Writing Project, which fails to include provisions for linguistic and cultural diversity (or language choice) and constructs all students in a way that erases the presence of Black students and students of color. Considering these omissions from WPA guiding documents, Perryman-Clark and Craig bring to our attention three programs—two at HBCUs, Spelman University and Huston-Tillotson University, and one at a PWI, Western Michigan University—as examples of Afrocentric orientations to writing curricula. The editors use these schools to build out a framework that coalesces into three principles that represent a Black perspective in WPA work: 1) Afrocentric pedagogical materials are placed at the center of the curriculum; 2) programmatic assessment measures are designed with Black student success in mind; and 3) successful writing programs understand that they can implement Afrocentric pedagogy and antiracist writing assessment practices and still support all students. These three tenets are built upon the lived experiences of the contributors and the successful work of writing programs showcased in the collection.

Perryman-Clark, Craig, and their contributors all point to dire moments in higher education in which writing program administrators make decisions about who to focus curriculum on, how to assess students, and how to treat each other as professionals. These are life and death battles. By centering Afrocentric and Black approaches to writing programs, WPAs combat White supremacist ways of being that insidiously show up in myths around writing, language, knowledge, instruction, and other aspects of education. Perryman-Clark and Craig have put together a succinct collection that directly challenges contemporary hegemonic writing instruction. They clearly affirm that those not willing to risk and lose the privilege they have accumulated as present-day WPAs need to make room for practitioners who seek to transform higher education through centering Black perspectives, Black students, and Black people. These ideas only take hold if WPAs become accomplices who can embody anti-racism in a way that Black bodies simply cannot; we need more White WPAs to be willing to take up Afrocentric frameworks in their classrooms, even if it means losing substantial privileges they have historically held. Consequently, this text is a must-read for anyone who hopes to do socially just writing program administration, wants to impact the lives of others in materially consequential ways, and desires generally to be a good person. Throughout, contributors explain that in order to work towards a socially just world, we must divest in the orientations that give us power and privilege over others. WPAs are in unique positions to reorient writing programs and, in turn, academia towards anti-racist Afrocentric futures.

East Lansing, Michigan

Rhetorical Feminism and This Thing Called Hope, by Cheryl Glenn. Carbondale: Southern Illinois UP, 2018. 273 pp.

Reviewed by Anne Turner, University of New Mexico

Historically, the dismissal of women's voices has created a culture of silence, preventing women from speaking at all, or, if they do speak, they may face social backlash. The public response to the #MeToo movement, with its prominence in the news and social media, is just one example of the impact of women's rhetorical power against silence. Rhetorical feminism—a method used to "disidentify" feminist rhetorical studies from "hegemonic rhetoric" (4)—develops an intersectional and inclusive space in rhetorical studies, despite the silencing of women in the historically masculinized canon (Hawkesworth 444; Glenn, "Rhetoric Retold" 2; Lunsford 6). As rhetorical feminism marches forward with hope, the need for scholarship that promotes the individual and collective voices of *all* women is crucial not only to academia, but also to the current political happenings in the world.

Rhetorical Feminism and This Thing Called Hope by Cheryl Glenn explores the multi-faceted dimensions of rhetorical feminism, interweaving the historical waves of feminist movements with rhetorical studies and recovery work. Her purpose is clear: to create a "guide" to rhetorical feminism (2) and solidify rhetorical feminism within the field of rhetorical studies as a "stance" that disidentifies "with hegemonic rhetoric" (4). She integrates the history of feminism within the United States from the 19th century onward, defines rhetorical feminism's methodology, examines issues of identity and activism, and presents theories of rhetorical feminist study from the 1970s forward. The poignant examples of women who embody rhetorical feminism, like Gloria Anzaldúa, establish the presence of the work within the field and a consciousness of intersectionality. *Rhetorical Feminism and This Thing Called Hope* is a vital read for anyone involved in researching, teaching, and/or mentoring within the fields of rhetoric, writing, and composition.

Glenn begins with an introduction outlining her purpose, focus, and each of the eight chapters. The first four chapters of the book reflect on the historical movements of rhetorical feminism and emerging methodologies and theories, using the work of authors and researchers in the field as illustrations. The final four chapters are dedicated to the practice of rhetorical feminism in the spheres of teaching, mentoring, and administrating.

In her first chapter ("Activism"), Glenn discusses the religious feminist rhetors of first-wave feminism called "Sister Rhetors" (6). These women, empowered by their positions of influence within the "quasi-public sphere" of religious organizations, became key orators of 19th century feminism (10).

They created numerous humanitarian organizations, established literacy education, and enacted social reform. Glenn names several key women—Maria W. Miller Stewart, Angelina Grimké, Lucretia Mott, Sojourner Truth—whose contributions led to the Women's Conventions of 1848 (Seneca, New York) and 1851 (Akron, Ohio). Their early rhetorical feminism included themes of disidentification, caring for the marginalized, respect for wisdom and experience, slavery and abolition, and gender inequality. This chapter effectively establishes the historical boundaries and roots of rhetorical feminism.

Glenn opens chapter two ("Identity") with her objective, "to make rhetorical studies more representative and inclusive," and focuses her writing on the identity politics of those allowed to speak, those allowed to speak for others, and the pressing question of "who merits an audience" (25). While referencing the second-wave of feminism of the 1960's and 70's, Glenn illustrates how "middle-class white heterosexual feminists failed rhetorically" (30) when they claimed to speak for all women, when they should have recognized intersectionality and addressed the diverse experiences and needs of women of color and the working class. The chapter concludes with a discussion of these issues in the third and fourth waves of the feminist movement (1990s and 2010s).

Rather than focus on individual theorists in chapter three ("Theories"), Glenn categorizes the work of several key rhetorical feminists: "disidentification, transformation at transaction, reconceptualization of rhetorical appeals, [and] expanded notions of delivery" (51). Rhetors (Anazaldúa, hooks, Daly, Starhawk) who influenced the category of disidentification wrote on themes of confronting racism and resistance while writing accessible prose. Transformation at transaction focuses on how feminist rhetors (Minh-ha, Foss and Griffin, Gearhart, Campbell) transformed rhetorical tools to meet their own purposes. In the final categories, Glenn expounds on these themes as they apply to discourse and argument. This approach effectively synthesizes the theoretical convergences of rhetorical feminism and speaks once again to Glenn's focus on intersectionality.

In chapter four ("Methods and Methodologies"), Glenn outlines methods and controversies of rhetorical feminist research. She distinguishes the importance of transparency in rhetorical feminism over traditional "objectivity" and emphasizes the focus of researchers' personal connection to their research subjects. With a goal of "helping to regender the study of rhetoric," Glenn cites Royster and Kirsch's foundational categories (critical imagination, strategic contemplation, social circulation, and globalization) as being key to the development of rhetorical feminism's methodologies (100). Historiography is another key methodology, but Glenn argues that the work produced from research within historiography must do more than interpret the past and recover "lost" rhetors. In order to change the field of rhetoric, it must also change "masculinist rhetorical studies" (103). Other methodologies for invigorating the field include historical research, ethnographic or "naturalistic" studies, and possibilities of future methods to transform the field (117).

"Teaching," chapter five, discusses the teaching tradition of rhetoric with the intersection of rhetorical feminist pedagogy and explores how such an approach can transform student retention. The most influential factor in student retention is a teacher who is skilled in the subject matter, a good communicator, and able to successfully develop course materials (130). Feminist pedagogy, Glenn argues, can provide hope for systemic change while authoritatively supporting students in the classroom through positionality, engagement, and ethics; feminist rhetorical pedagogy can also nurture this hope when an instructor uses historical and political feminist texts. Glenn concludes this chapter with a demonstration of feminist pedagogies at work.

In addition to teaching, the rhetorical tradition also carries with it a history of mentoring. In chapter six ("Mentoring"), Glenn describes the characteristics of an effective feminist mentor and the various methodologies associated with feminist mentoring—some of which include disidentifying with the masculine, hierarchical modeling of mentoring, and committing to equality. She explains that "the goal of mentoring is a relationship" and that women often seek out "mutual mentoring" where mentor and mentee talk, listen, and support each other as they break down hierarchies of power (155). Glenn acknowledges that while a fully-invested mentor is crucial, taking on too many mentees can challenge relationship dynamics and create affective labor (170). With proper attention to the needs of the mentor and mentee, these relationships generate hope for productive relationships through empowering interactions that can open up professional opportunities for all involved.

In chapter seven ("Writing Program Administration"), Glenn addresses the unique history of writing programs and the contributions that feminists make and have made to pedagogy, curriculum, and administration in those spaces. She confronts the powers and limitations of WPA work, demonstrating moments when women are "pushed to the margins" by a masculine academy that views the profession of teaching and administrating English as women's work (177). While a WPA can "actively work against that code," Glenn demonstrates that as an administrator, a feminist will also need to navigate and perform according to the system they are in. She shares her own experience working as a WPA at Penn State University, along with the difficult decisions she had to make providing adequate classes without overburdening contingent faculty.

Finally, in chapter eight ("This Thing Called Hope"), Glenn outlines the future potential of rhetorical feminism as she reflects on the current political discord in the United States. The hope for a woman to "shatter the presidential glass ceiling" is tempered with the concerns of those who would listen when she speaks, given the historical marginalization of women (197). She warns that division and exclusivity amongst feminists will worsen the "splintering" and inhibit the work of politics and rhetoric (200). She calls on all to "bridge serious differences" in fields of study and activism (204). In the end, Glenn concludes that an engaged, connected, inclusive, and intersectional approach to rhetorical feminism is worth working towards to build a future in which *all* voices are listened to, and where *all* are committed to feminism within the political and social spheres.

Glenn's work is simultaneously inspirational and inciting. The implications of her writing reveal that despite the forward momentum of rhetorical feminism, the same needs have existed since the beginning: the need to listen to the diversity of women's voices and understand women's needs. In order for this movement to grow, feminists (of all genders and colors) need to be present in their research and conversations with the intent to include and build bridges so that we may all continue to march forward—with hope.

Albuquerque, New Mexico

Works Cited

Glenn, Cheryl. *Rhetoric Retold: Regendering the Tradition From Antiquity Through the Renaissance*. Southern Illinois University Press, 1997.

Hawkesworth, Mary E. "Feminist Rhetoric: Discourses on the Male Monopoly of Thought." *Political Theory*, vol. 16, no. 3, 1988, pp. 444–67. *JSTOR*, www.jstor.org/stable/191581. Accessed 15 Feb. 2020.

Lunsford, Andrea A. "On Reclaiming Rhetorica." *Reclaiming Rhetorica: Women in the Rhetorical Tradition*, University of Pittsburgh Press, 1995.

Next Steps: New Directions for/in Writing about Writing, edited by Barbara Bird, Doug Downs, I. Moriah McCracken, and Jan Rieman. University Press of Colorado, 2019. 306 pp.

Reviewed by John H. Whicker, Fontbonne University

Next Steps: New Directions for/in Writing about Writing provides an expansive look at the increasingly popular Writing about Writing (WAW) approach to teaching writing. As the editors state, the collection reveals "the breadth of current WAW approaches" in order to "extend the representation of this 'thing' that has come to be called writing about writing" (3, 271). The collection does not taxonomize the approaches presented or offer explicit guidelines for best practices. Instead, the editors argue that WAW is neither a pedagogy, suggesting particular "techniques or practices in the classroom," nor a curriculum, mandating reading or writing assignments, but an "approach" that the contributors apply differently in many institutional contexts (3). The collection, then, provides a multitude of assignments, courses, programs, and possibilities, creating, "a deep repository of images of student learning through contemporary WAW approaches" (272).

Bird et al. set out three foundational principles for WAW approaches:

- Writing is the content of the course that students' study and write about;
- The course treats students as writers not "*student* writers;" and
- Instructors generate knowledge about writing "*with* their students not *for* them" (3–4).

These principles do not include the reading of writing studies scholarship that has been a hallmark of WAW in the past, seeming to leave the door open to using readings that are less than full academic articles. In the first chapter, however, the editors *do* reiterate the benefits of reading difficult scholarly texts, suggesting some preference for this prior staple of WAW courses.

The editors argue that approaches to WAW "might be impossible to taxonomize" (18), so it is no wonder that the organization of the chapters might seem somewhat unclear. Based on the three WAW principles above, they divide the book into three sections correlated to three desired outcomes: developing *writerly identities*, mindful and individual *processes*, and *engagement* with writing knowledge and students' own learning and transfer. Readers will notice considerable overlap among these outcomes and may struggle to see distinctions among the sections or consistency among the chapters in each section. In many ways, however, the ambiguous organization of contributions reiterates the larger goal of the collection: to highlight the significant variety of WAW approaches. The order of chapters is engaging: the variety of approaches, methods, styles, and lengths readers encounter from chapter to chapter helps provide a better reading experience than had the editors sought to group chapters by more definitive similarities.

Three chapters present important historical or theoretical context for WAW: Bird, Downs, McCracken, and Rieman provide a brief history of WAW; Wardle and Adler-Kassner review recent scholarship on threshold concepts as they relate to WAW approaches; and Nowacek reviews writing transfer, which both the editors and many contributors assert is the primary goal of WAW approaches.

The twenty-six remaining chapters of *Next Steps* give a variety of accounts about particular WAW programs, courses, assignments, or experiences at a wide variety of institutional contexts—from a 550-student engineering program in Qatar to a 63,000-student R1 university in the US. While most describe first-year writing courses, others detail professional, advanced, and basic writing courses and one even highlights a professional writing major.

Contributions are relatively short, with "vignettes" of three to eight pages and longer contributions averaging around ten to twelve. Chapters are first and foremost accounts of the contributors' experiences with WAW and descriptions of the assignments, courses, and programs they have developed and implemented. Though some authors report on research methodologies that drive empirical inquiry, the brevity of the chapters and the primacy of describing how WAW is being used programmatically suggests that we might best read these chapters as reflections. While many chapters do include some qualitative evidence to support the authors' claims regarding the benefits of WAW, many of the assertions, particularly regarding metacognition and transfer, seem to rely more on theory, teacher experience, and optimism than empirical data. That said, many chapters seem to imply that fuller accounts of research that more firmly supports the reflections and discussions in *Next Steps* may be forthcoming.

The space of a short review inhibits a full review of all of the contributions to *Next Steps*, but there are themes that emerge among many of the chapters, and some of the unique contributions are worth mentioning.

The majority of contributions describe WAW approaches that focus primarily on readings and assignments that help students learn to research and analyze writing contexts. These contributors focus on teaching students to transfer writing knowledge by teaching them to identify and analyze differences and similarities in communities of practice and genres (Arbor; Cutrufello; di Gennaro; Johnson; LaRiviere; Lucchesi; Mahaffey and Rieman; Ogilvie; Read and Michaud; Robinson; Wenger). Most of these focus on concepts such as discourse communities, activity systems, ecologies, or genre. Di Gennaro has students read both composition and applied linguistics scholarship, focusing the entire course on similarities and differences of academic writing among students' various disciplinary majors with a fine-tuned attention to features and patterns of academic language. Di Gennaro's chapter is also interesting because, in contrast to the editors, she presents her chapter as a how-to guide for implementing a WAW course and makes the contentious claim that writing about writing should not entail students writing about their own writing. She is also critical of teachers who approach WAW in ways she views as expressivist, which puts her at odds with many of her fellow contributors who do just that.

Approaches that primarily ask students to write about and analyze their own past and present writing and language experiences are the other most common contribution (Aksakalova and Zino; Grant; Hart; Hoover, et al.; Kleinfeld; Smith, Frick, and Siebel; Wilson, Jackson, and Vera). Christina Grant's account of her attempts to help multilingual international students at a top Canadian R1 institution "reestablish their voices and roles" is most clearly an example of the very expressive process pedagogy that di Gennaro critiques. Grant introduces students to scholarship on process, voice, identity, and language to help students develop self-efficacy as experts on their own writing by being empowered with language and research from writing studies.

Others focus their students' attention not on process but on experiences of language and literacy more broadly. Wilson, Jackson, and Vera's WAW assignment sequence for a non-WAW basic writing course asks students to research their literacy and language experience through translingual scholarship. This approach, because of the focus on the social nature of language, seems to move away from a solely self-focused project toward more context-oriented assignments, but comes short of context analysis. This is even more evident in Tremain or Casey's chapters, which use the social nature of language to bridge these two broad foci, asking students first to attend to their own process or language experiences but then also to connect what they learn to issues of disciplinarity. Casey describes assignments that attend to process and literacy but also ones that ask students to investigate disciplinary literacy practices. All these scholars, however, focus primarily on dispositions and self-efficacy, which Tremain in particular notes may be necessary for transfer.

Many of the contributions that focus on students' own experiences describe basic writing and FYW courses for international and other multilingual student populations, while context analysis assignments are commonly reported in FYW and professional writing courses. This suggests that there is room for further research on how these different types of assignments impact diverse students in different course contexts.

Some chapters add depth to WAW's possibilities by connecting it to gamification (Stinson), multimodality (Wenger), and podcasting (Smith, Frick, and Siebel). LaRiviere advises readers on how to integrate WAW into seemingly rigid non-WAW standardized curricula. Mahaffey and Rieman describe designing and implementing a program-wide WAW curriculum inclusively with instructors from non-writing studies backgrounds. Bryan, Roozen, and Stack also reflect on their efforts to help diverse stakeholders become comfortable with WAW. deWinter describes revising the curriculum of a professional writing major using WAW principles. Two chapters, one by Gaier and Wallace and the other by Sugimoto, are student reflections, the authors all former students in WAW courses who describe how they have benefited from their experiences.

Next Steps is a truly broad look at the wide diversity of WAW approaches. This diversity, however, could be overwhelming. Readers looking for some guidance in deciding what concepts might be most important to teach, or what readings or assignments might best teach them, will finish this collection with many more options but few directions for making decisions about how to spend limited class time. *Next Steps* has certainly shown WAW's diversity, but further work is still needed to determine whether some WAW approaches might be better for different student audiences than others.

St. Louis, Missouri

Contributors

Christopher J. Barber is currently a doctoral student in rhetoric and composition at Purdue University. His research interests include transfer theory, rhetorical ethics, argumentation theory, and how these fields may positively inform and shape composition pedagogy.

Hannah Bellwoar is Associate Professor of English and the Director of Writing at Juniata College, where she teaches professional and digital writing. Her research interests include digital literacies, undergraduate research in writing studies, and usability studies. Her work has been published in *Kairos*, *Harlot*, *OneShot*, and *Technical Communication Quarterly*.

Kristine L. Blair is Dean of the McAnulty College and Graduate School of Liberal Arts and a Professor of English at Duquesne University. She serves as Editor of *Computers and Composition*.

Courtney Buck attends Wittenberg University in Springfield, Ohio. She is an undergraduate double major in English and communication with a journalism minor. She enjoys working in the writing center and has presented at the 2019 ECWCA and IWCA-NCPTW conferences with her co-researchers. Courtney also attended the 2019 Naylor Workshop for Undergraduate Researchers.

Dominic DelliCarpini is the Naylor Endowed Professor Writing Studies and Dean of the Center for Community Engagement at York College of Pennsylvania. He also served as WPA for thirteen years. He founded the Naylor Workshop on Undergraduate Research in Writing Studies, and his areas of research include writing and civic engagement, writing program administration, and undergraduate research.

Sue Fletcher is a fellow of the Ohio University Appalachian Writing Project and has taught first-year composition for a number of years. Sue is currently employed as the curriculum coordinator for the first-year programming office at Ohio University and pursuing her PhD in rhetoric and composition.

Anne Ruggles Gere is Authur Thurnau Professor of English and Gertrude Buck Professor of Education at the University of Michigan, where she serves as chair of the joint PhD in English and Education.

Pennie L. Gray is Associate Professor of Educational Studies at Illinois Wesleyan University, where she teaches courses in composition, language arts, literacy, children's literature, and pedagogy.

Alex Hanson is a PhD candidate in composition and cultural rhetoric at Syracuse University. Her research interests include feminist rhetorics, multilingual writing instruction, writing program administration, institutional rhetoric and policy, and single moms in academia.

Lizzie Hutton is Assistant Professor of English and Director of the Howe Writing Center at Miami University, Ohio. Her work has appeared in journals including *WPA*, *College English*, and the *Journal of English Linguistics*.

David Johnson is an advanced doctoral candidate in rhetoric and composition at Ohio University. His areas of specialization include antiracist composition pedagogies, rhetorics of race, writing center studies, and qualitative composition research.

Kristine Johnson is Associate Professor of English at Calvin College where she directs the written rhetoric program and teaches courses in composition pedagogy, linguistics, and first-year writing. With J. Michael Rifenburg, she is editing a special issue of *Pedagogy* (2021) on undergraduate research in English Studies.

Anna V. Knutson serves as Assistant Professor of English and Director of First-Year Writing at Duquesne University. Interested in writing program administration, writing knowledge transfer, and digital literacies, Anna is currently exploring the roles of genre and multimodality in writing knowledge transfer across domains among intersectional feminist college students.

Rebecca Lorimer Leonard is Associate Professor of English at the University of Massachusetts, Amherst where she teaches undergraduate and graduate courses on language diversity, literacy studies, and research methods.

Courtney A. Mauck is a PhD student in rhetoric and composition at Ohio University. Her research is primarily focused on social media, multimodal composition, and first-year writing pedagogy, though she is also interested in game studies, accessibility, and learning transfer.

Katrina L. Miller teaches rhetoric and composition courses in the Core Writing Program and English Department at the University of Nevada, Reno. She is also the Assistant Director of the Core Writing Program. Her research focuses on programmatic writing assessment and developmental writing.

Jessie L. Moore is the Director of the Center for Engaged Learning and Professor of English at Elon University. Jessie leads the Center's research seminars, which support multi-institutional inquiry on engaged learning topics.

Her publications include *Excellence in Mentoring Undergraduate Research* (co-edited with Maureen Vandermaas-Peeler and Paul Miller, CUR, 2018).

Emily Nolan is a second-year undergraduate English major and journalism minor at Wittenberg University. She has presented her analysis of asynchronous eTutoring alongside her co-researchers at the 2019 ECWCA writing center conference, the 2019 Naylor workshop for undergraduate researchers, and the 2019 IWCA-NCPTW international writing center conference.

Michael Pak is Assistant Professor of English at the University of Hawai'I – West O'ahu, where he also serves as the Writing Program Coordinator. His research interests include composition pedagogy, rhetoric, critical theory, and popular culture.

Justine Post is Assistant Professor of Rhetoric and Composition and the Writing Center Director at Ohio Northern University. Her research explores student and instructor experiences in the writing classroom with a focus on student support services, instructor feedback, and writing development.

Floyd Pouncil is a PhD student in the Writing, Rhetoric, and American Cultures program at Michigan State University. Their work focuses on understanding, honoring, and utilizing multiple literacies to design and implement systems in higher education to support students, faculty, and staff towards socially responsible personal, professional, and institutional goals.

Jill Palmer is from Alexandria, Pennsylvania and graduated in December 2019 from Juniata College with an undergraduate degree in professional writing and digital media. A member of Sigma Tau Delta, her academic interests include digital writing and film studies. In her free time, she enjoys writing creatively, drawing, painting, and reading.

Danielle Pappo is a PhD student in composition and rhetoric at the University of Massachusetts, Amherst, where she also teaches first-year writing and tutors at the writing center.

Kyle Piscioniere is a PhD student, the Assistant Director of the writing center, and a writing instructor at the University of Massachusetts, Amherst.

J. Michael Rifenburg works at the University of North Georgia. Nationally, he serves on the CCCC Committee on Undergraduate Research. With Kristine Johnson, he is editing a special issue of *Pedagogy* (2021) on undergraduate research in English Studies.

Ryan P. Shepherd is Assistant Professor of English at Ohio University. His research interests include learning transfer theory, social media, and multimodal composing. His work has appeared in *Computers & Composition*, *Kairos*, *The Journal of Multimodal Rhetorics*, and *The Journal of Response to Writing*.

Jody Shipka is Associate Professor at the University of Maryland, Baltimore County. She is the author of *Toward a Composition Made Whole* and her work has appeared in *College Composition and Communication*, *College English*, *Computers and Composition*, *enculturation*, *Kairos*, *Text and Talk*, *Writing Selves/Writing Societies*, and other edited collections.

Naomi Silver is Associate Director of the Sweetland Center for Writing at the University of Michigan. Her research focuses on multimodal writing, electronic portfolios, and reflection in digital contexts. She is chair of the CCCC Committee on Computers in Composition and Communication and co-directs the Sweetland Digital Rhetoric Collaborative.

Jamie Spallino is an undergraduate English major and women's studies minor at Wittenberg University. In addition to tutoring at Wittenberg's Writing Center, she has presented alongside co-researchers at ECWCA 2019 and IWCA-NCPTW 2019, and she attended the 2019 Naylor Workshop for Undergraduate Researchers.

Nathaniel Street is Assistant Professor of English and writing program coordinator at Mount Saint Vincent University. He writes on the inventive and pedagogical power of writing and rhetoric in a posthuman sense. He would like to thank John Muckelbauer, Christy Friend, and Larissa Atkison for their thoughtful feedback and gracious support.

Fisher Stroud is from Washington, DC and is currently an undergraduate senior at Juniata College in Huntingdon, PA. She is working on her senior thesis film, *She Is*, which examines the director's gaze as an unreliable narrator in film.

Sarah Swofford is Assistant Professor of Composition and Rhetoric and Writing Program Administrator in the Department of English, Theater, and Interdisciplinary Studies at the University of South Carolina Beaufort. She researches issues related to writing development, particularly those related to rural education and transitions to college writing.

Sandra L. Tarabochia is Associate Professor of English at the University of Oklahoma. Her scholarship has advanced a pedagogical ethic for cross-curricular literacy work, explored methodological innovations for studying writing through the lifespan, and examined emotional labor in the context of emerging scholars mentoring relationships.

Anne Turner is a Core Writing Co-Coordinator and a Teaching Assistant at the University of New Mexico. Her research interests include writing program administration, composition pedagogy, multilingual writers in composition classrooms, and digital media literacy.

John Whicker is the Director of Composition, Assistant Professor in Professional Writing at Fontbonne University in Saint Louis, and co-coordinator of the Writing about Writing Development Standing Group of the Conference on College Composition and Communication.

Improve Your Writing Course
From Sentences to Social Practices

How Students Write: A Linguistic Analysis

By Laura Louise Aull

6 × 9 • 230 pp.

Paper $34.00
$27.20 with code HSW20

Cloth $65.00
$52.00 with code HSW20

Offer expires 30 November 2020

Writing Changes: Alphabetic Text and Multimodal Composition

Edited by Pegeen Reichert Powell

6 × 9 • 322 pp.

Paper $34.00
$27.20 with code WC20

Cloth $80.00
$64.00 with code WC20

Offer expires 30 September 2020

mla.org/books   bookorders@mla.org   646 576-5161

Join the MLA today and save 30% on all MLA titles.

PARLOR PRESS
EQUIPMENT FOR LIVING

New Releases

The Naylor Report on Undergraduate Research in Writing Studies edited by Dominic DelliCarpini, Jenn Fishman, and Jane Greer

Internationalizing the Writing Center: A Guide for Developing a Multilingual Writing Center by Noreen Lape

Socrates at Verse and Other Philosophical Poems by Christopher Norris

Writing Spaces: Readings on Writing Volume 3 edited by Dana Driscoll, Mary Stewart, and Matthew Vetter

Off the Page: Literary and Cultural Criticism as Multimedia Performance by Tom Lavazzi

Forthcoming

Collaborative Writing Playbook: An Instructor's Guide to Designing Writing Projects for Student Teams by Joe Moses and Jason Tham

The Art of Public Writing by Zachary Michael Jack

Check Out Our New Website!

Discounts, open access titles, instant ebook downloads, and more.

And new series:

Comics and Graphic Narratives. Series Editors: Sergio Figueiredo, Jason Helms, and Anastasia Salter

Inkshed: Writing Studies in Canada. Series Editors: Heather Graves and Roger Graves

www.parlorpress.com

Composition Studies **Discount:** Use COMPSTUDIES20 at checkout to receive a 20% discount on all titles not on sale through August 15, 2020.